ARTICLE 36

of the
Belgic Confession

VINDICATED

aga
Dr. Abraha

A Critique of His Series on
Church and State in
Common Grace

DR. P. J. HOEDEMAKER

PANTOCRATOR PRESS

WORDBRIDGE PUBLISHING

Aalten, the Netherlands

www.wordbridge.net

Dutch original: Dr. P. J. Hoedemaker, *Artikel XXXVI onzer Nederduitsche Geloofsbelijdenis tegenover Dr. A. Kuyper gehandhaafd: beoordelingen van de opstellen in de "Heraut" over kerk en staat* (Amsterdam: Van Dam, 1901).

ISBN 978–90–76660–52–3

TABLE OF CONTENTS

PREFACE

Who was Hoedemaker?[1]

Philippus Jacobus Hoedemaker (1839–1910) was a leading figure in the tumultuous late-19th-early-20th century Dutch ecclesiastical landscape. Born in 1839 into a Separated Reformed ("Afgescheiden Gereformeerde") church family – interesting in view of the fact that his subsequent career would be conducted within the "established" national church – Hoedemaker spent his teen and college-age years in the United States, where his family moved in 1852. He studied theology for three years at the Congregationalist college in Chicago (again noteworthy considering his future ecclesiastical orientation), during which time he supported himself by preaching, for which, it was acknowledged on all sides, he had a gift.

Hoedemaker returned to Europe in 1861 to complete his education, in 1867 graduating *magna cum laude* from Utrecht University with a doctorate in divinity, by virtue of a dissertation entitled *Het Probleem der Vrijheid en het Theïstisch Godsbegrip* [The Problem of Freedom and the Theistic Concept of God].[2] In the dedication he makes mention of a surprise figure, Ralph Waldo Emerson. First he quotes him:

Profounder, profounder mans [*sic*] spirit must dive,
To his aye rolling orbit, no goal will arrive,
The heavens which now draw him, with sweetness untold
Once found, for new heavens he leaveth the old.

after which follows the dedication proper:

---

[1] Sources in addition to those quoted below: Scheers, *Philippus Jacobus Hoedemaker;* de Bie and Loosjes, *Biographisch woordenboek*, pp. 51ff.; *Dr. Ph. J. Hoedemaker 1868-1908: Gedenkboek Ter Gelegenheid Van Zijn 40-Jarige Ambtsbediening* [Commemorative Book on the 40th Anniversary of Dr. Hoedemaker's Service].

[2] Published in Amsterdam by H. Höveker, 1867.

RALPH WALDO EMERSON,

POET AND THINKER.
FOR HIS KIND APPRECIATION OF MY BOYISH EFFORTS,
AND THE IMPETUS HE HAS GIVEN TOWARDS MY STUDIES,
AS WELL AS THE INFLUENCE HE HAS HAD ON MY MIND,
THIS WORK IS RESPECTFULLY INSCRIBED BY

THE AUTHOR.

Hoedemaker's orientation towards philosophy thus came as no surprise. Emerson had sat in on one of his school presentations "and immediately saw something special in him."[3] A broad philosophical and cultural interest accompanied his ecclesiastical and theological endeavors throughout his life. His stay in America also had an enduring effect on his outlook. "In all circumstances his mind retained something of the breadth of the forests and plains of America. Dutch popular piety and American cultural openness remained united in him. Something of the adventurous daring enterprise of the colonists intersected with his loyalty to the piety that he inherited, in particular from his mother."[4]

Indeed, it was his mother who prophesied that one day he would return to the fatherland and labor for the restoration of *Neerlands kerk*.[5] Hoedemaker eventually made good on this prophecy, although only by more or less stumbling into it. As he related the story, upon arriving in the Netherlands he was invited to preach in two different congregations in Amsterdam, one a national Reformed, one a Separated Reformed. He accepted both invitations. But the separatist church, upon hearing of his acceptance of an invitation to preach in the national church, revoked its invitation. In this he discerned an indication of the direction his career should take.[6]

---

[3] Scheers, *Philippus Jacobus Hoedemaker*, p. 9.

[4] *Ibid.*

[5] Hoedemaker, *Na Een-en-Dertig Jaren* [After 31 Years] (sermon delivered on February 19th, 1893), pp. 10–11.

[6] *Ibid.,* pp. 8–9.

Hoedemaker's career as minister of the Word began in 1868 in Veenendaal with a call to the national church congregation there. This was followed by turns in Rotterdam (1873) and Amsterdam (1876).

During his period in Veenendaal, Hoedemaker befriended Abraham Kuyper, and in 1880 he accepted a position at the new Free University. But his differences with Kuyper and his followers would speedily become apparent. The immediate cause was Kuyper's exodus from the national church to form a separate denomination. Hoedemaker fought this movement with might and main. But his divergence was more than ecclesiastical. Hoedemaker opposed the so-called Neocalvinist agenda at its core, viewing it as a further development of the Revolution, precisely what it was supposed to combat.

Not that he disagreed with Kuyper's basic agenda, to bring the lordship of Christ to bear in every area of life. On the contrary: it was Kuyper's purported betrayal of that goal which instigated the rupture. Hoedemaker shared the original purpose of the Free University, "which takes the Bible as the unconditional basis on which to rear the whole structure of human knowledge in every department of life,"[7] thus promoting science formed by Scripture and Confession, with theology restored as the "queen of the sciences." Kuyper's deviation from this program is precisely what Hoedemaker criticized (see below, "About this book").

After his break with Kuyper, Hoedemaker returned to the pulpit, first in Frisia (Nijland, two years) and then Amsterdam, where he would lead the consolidation of the orthodox Reformed within the national church. He did this through various channels while always striving to remain above party formation, which he considered the curse of the modern age. In this effort, his publishing career paralleled that of Kuyper's, although without approaching K.'s sheer volume. He published a range of books and pamphlets criticizing the Nonconformist movement, and he began editing a weekly church-oriented newspaper, *The Reformed Church* ("De Gereformeerde Kerk") in 1888, as a counterweight to Kuyper's *The Herald*. Interesting here is his choice of title. Kuyper had appropriated the term "Gereformeerd," the original designation of the Dutch Reformed church before it officially became the "Hervormde" church in 1816, for

---

[7] Kuyper, *Lectures on Calvinism,* p. i.

his splinter church. In response, Hoedemaker was sending the message that "Gereformeerd" was not the private property of the Nonconformists, but was the patrimonial title of the Dutch Reformed generally. Both *Article 36* and *Reformed Ecclesiology in an Age of Denominationalism* were written in this light.

Beyond his writings on ecclesiology and church-state issues, Hoedemaker penned significant works on biblical theology, including a comprehensive critique of higher criticism.

Perhaps most important of all, Hoedemaker spawned a movement in favor of the national church and the heritage of the Christian state which gained many adherents and exerted profound influence on the development of Dutch theology, the national church, and Christian political action. Perhaps the most important of his votaries was Prof. A. A. van Ruler (1908–1960).

Hoedemaker suffered a light stroke in 1907, which restricted but did not put an end to his preaching career (as witness the autobiographical sermon *De Nood Ons Opgelegd* [Forced by Necessity], delivered on January 16th, 1908, and his retirement sermon, *De Sabbat om de Mensch* [The Sabbath was Made for Man], August 30th, 1909). He passed away on July 26th, 1910.

About this book

Hoedemaker shared the original goals of the Free University and its parent, the Association for Higher Education on a Reformed Basis. These goals reflecting the Reformed basis revolved around 1) establishing a Scriptural basis for science, thus restoring the role of a Scripture-based theology as queen of the sciences, with the other disciplines taking the theological baselines into account, and 2) recognizing the Three Forms of Unity, including the Belgic Confession of Faith, as the expression of that Scriptural basis of knowledge – with the ever-present necessity continually to test those doctrinal standards against Scripture.

Test the doctrinal standards against Scripture: this was precisely Hoedemaker's issue with Kuyper. For the latter based his entire agenda in church and state on the rejection of Article 36 of the Belgic Confession, without, however, ever having provided a sufficient Scriptural warrant for doing so.

The third clause of Article 36, "On Magistrates," reads as follows: "And their office is, not only to have regard unto and watch for the welfare of the civil state, but also that they protect the sacred ministry, and thus may remove and prevent all idolatry and false worship; that the kingdom of antichrist may be thus destroyed, and the kingdom of Christ promoted. They must, therefore, countenance the preaching of the word of the gospel every where, that God may be honored and worshiped by every one, as he commands in his Word."[8] By all appearances, it is this section, apparently so thoroughly out of touch with modernity, which needed to be removed, not "idolatry and false worship." But things were not as simple as that, argued Hoedemaker. Much more was at stake than the mere excision of an errant clause. In fact, implicit in such an apparently simple and restricted modification was wide-ranging deviation, indeed a different confession altogether, making a *comprehensive* revision of the Confession necessary. Furthermore, such an action needed to be taken in thorough consultation with Scripture, by the church assembled. Neither of these conditions was met.

This is the burden of Hoedemaker's argument. Kuyper and his followers had, on their own, adopted a different confession without acknowledging the fact. As Hoedemaker put it to A. F. de Savornin Lohman, Kuyper's comrade-in-arms in the church split which created the Nonconformist "Gereformeerde" churches, the difference between them lay not merely in one clause of Article 36, but in their Confession generally. "One and the same Confession?" asked Hoedemaker in a pamphlet of the same name.[9] For him, the appeal to the Three Forms of Unity rang hollow. "It is precisely for this reason that I wholeheartedly reject the principle of your so-called Reformation etc., and your appeal to the Three Forms of Unity, in connection with the local church or the churches which, under this erroneous and misleading principle, were later brought together under an apparently Reformed church government" (below, p. 16). The change in confession regarding the state had this movement to Nonconformity as its logical consequence. The church split "took place under cover of a false principle – neutrality" (p. 16), the same principle behind the abandonment of Article 36.

The false principle runs through everything in the Kuyperian system. It affects the arrangement of the state and law: "the deviation from the Confession results in a deviation in the science connected with it. Article 36 contains the

---

[8] See n. 49, p. 36.

[9] See n. 26, p. 16.

architectonic principle according to which a corresponding system of civil punishment, and any other right, must be set up" (p. 8).

It shakes the entire scientific edifice in its foundation, affecting all the faculties. "If it is from the Confession that the principles are derived which determine the source, the material, and the direction of a science, any deviation from the Confession must, as has already been pointed out, become visible in the science under its influence. It follows again that, under the existing circumstances, church and state in particular and, more specifically, dogmatics as well as church law and state law, get more or less reconstructed under this influence" (p. 9).

It undermines Scripture itself. Kuyper's method affected the normativity, the perspicuity, and the sufficiency of Scripture, three key elements of Reformed doctrine. The normativity of Scripture is factually negated (p. 73). The perspicuity of Scripture is undermined by the idea that the civil magistrate is incapable of understanding the Word of God as it impinges on his duty (pp. 74ff.). The sufficiency of Scripture is gutted by the assertion that next to nothing is contained in Scripture that gives any direction at all with regard to civil government and affairs of state.

> You learn from this how wrong "the common understanding is, as if the government derives the light for its task from the Bible." It is made clear to you that "Scripture is not a book of recipes for which an index could be drawn up to find a ready answer to every question that crops up." And, after having attacked various and sundry standpoints that no one is defending, and defending what no one is attacking, you hear that for most people the Bible is a closed book. A closed book, either because they do not possess it, or because they do not understand it, or because those who are considered to understand it are divided amongst themselves, so that the poor magistrate is like Buridan's ass, stuck between two equidistant bunches of hay, standing immobile because he does not know which to choose (p. 80).

The doctrine of Scripture is connected with Kuyper's doctrine of common grace. Here, the principle of neutrality is hidden behind the façade of natural theology and "the natural knowledge of God." Hoedemaker was having none of it.

What, then, are we to understand by that "common grace" [Gemeene Gratie], about which we have been able to read for months on end in *The Herald*? And what is it supposed to mean when one reads in this weekly paper that the civil government acts by the light of common grace [gemeene gratie] and the church is the institute of particular grace [particuliere gratie]? In what relation does this grace stand to the general and special knowledge of God, general and special revelation, common and particular grace [genade]? One finds here an opposition which the Reformers did not accept, because it is at bottom Anabaptist; the sharp contradiction between nature and grace [genade], the kingdom of God and the kingdom of the world (p. 78).

In this understanding, the state is relegated to the sphere of common grace, which coincides with the "natural," as opposed to the "revealed," knowledge of God. This division of spheres is the reason why the magistrate is unable to understand the revealed will of God.

For this cause the non-confessing magistrate is authorized and obligated, in a complete and direct sense, to take the first (natural) knowledge of God as official guideline for its action, not the second (revealed).

The latter would only be the case if an extraordinary power, a supernatural organ existed to discern with firm assurance in every case what the revealed knowledge of God demands (p. 50).

And what is true of the non-confessing magistrate is true of the confessing magistrate as well, because there is no such thing as a confessing magistrate! "We thus have before us a curious viewpoint: the magistrate is God's servant, but the servant is incapable and consequently incompetent to investigate and implement the will of the Lord" (p. 54).

This is not all. Kuyper combines this with an insufficient concept of the church, whereby the church in its essence is confused with empirical existing manifestations thereof. This enables him to shift the real issue in Article 36 away from true and false *religion*, to the civil government's incapacity to decide between the various Christian denominations as to which is the true *church*. "Is it not evident how inappropriate, and how much in conflict with the entire conception of our fathers, it is to equate the true church with some denomination? Does Article 36 teach that it is not the Reformed religion, but this or that church form, which is to be considered the mark of the true church?" (p. 60).

Kuyper had been driven to this misunderstanding of the issue by his own action in leading the church schism. He and his followers characterized the national church as a false church, in order to justify that schism. It follows naturally that in a world of churches in which only one is the true one, the magistrate cannot choose between them. But that is to misconstrue the issue, and Kuyper did so not only for political gain but to obscure the damage he did to the church broadly construed.

Finally, after confusing true and false religion with the true and false church, Kuyper confuses freedom of religion with freedom of *conscience*. As Hoedemaker points out, "Calvin is said to have advocated violence in matters of faith. There is nothing, or nearly nothing, to this. We will consult the aforementioned treatise about it. Should the author – may it never be! – prove to have understood Calvin properly on this point, then perhaps we will be given a statement regarding that which continues to be a mystery to us, namely, his sympathy, even in politics, for Calvinism" (p. 40). In Kuyper's reading, freedom of conscience, which was championed against Rome, was cast aside when it came to Article 36, which supposedly codified coercion of conscience. But the Reformed church *always stood for freedom of conscience*. Kuyper confused freedom of conscience with freedom of religion. And this problem not only afflicted Kuyper, but contemporary Reformed believers generally:

> We fear the application of Reformed principles because we do not, or, if we do, we only barely distinguish between freedom of conscience and freedom of religion, equate it with the freedom to propagandize for our notions, equate this freedom with the freedom to slander, and confuse these four kinds of freedom with the theory of the Revolution, that the civil government as such may have no conviction, which is the reason why it may not recognize any church as the true one (p. 120).

The issue, then, is not whether heretics are to be punished by the state. After all, Kuyper himself recognized the need to punish blasphemy (see p. 122). This is always the way the issue is cast, to get public opinion immediately on one's side (see p. 15). Rather, the issue is this: which religion will be acknowledged as the touchstone of truth in the commonwealth, and, corollary to that, which will be tolerated (p. 121)?

Here is what it is not:

> The "removal and prevention of heresy and false religion" of which the Confession speaks, therefore has nothing to do with Christian churches and sects separated from each other in this way or that, but with entirely different groups which, through their godless positions or what our fathers considered to be such, infringe on the honor of God. It presupposes the freedom discussed above, which is inseparable from the national Reformed church's viewpoint regarding faith and the work of the Holy Spirit.
>
> The expression just quoted therefore not only can but must be restricted to public life, the sphere to be reckoned to the civil government (p. 122).

By what standard is the state to govern? By what law is its law to be judged? That standard is the Word of God, and if the state is incompetent to understand that Word, and agnostic with regard to religious truth and falsehood, then it is delivered over to the forces of secularism and power politics.

We have totally lost sight of this. "Remove and prevent" seems to apply only to the church these days. But this has consequences.

> Should one wish "to keep the church out of it," if one separates the church from the state, there are only three conceivable options: either the state has its own religion elevated above divisions of faith, or it becomes an atheist state and eliminates everything Christian from all public institutions, or it leaves legislation to chance, i.e., the momentary majority (p. 133; cf. also p. 108).

In our times we enjoy the dubious privilege of witnessing the state attempt all three of these expedients, in various synthetic and syncretistic combinations.

The public square is not a matter of indifference to the church. Its having been abandoned by an "enlightened" Christianity was the reason for the abject demoralization we see all around us.

> Have we, that is to say, has not our people visibly declined in every respect? Our resilience is paralyzed, our church divided, the national character of the Christian school is lost, the center of gravity of movement has shifted from the church to "the association for higher education," "the Central Committee," "Patrimonium [Christian labor union]," in a word, to the ballot box, the ideal of our living and striving has vanished! When the apostle Paul stood on the Areopagus and gained a few adherents for the truth he proclaimed, he was addressing the people as a whole. But according to Kuyper's system, on the cardinal issues we act in the interest of a group, an institute, an association (p. 117).

But when issues of church and state are brought back into their proper perspective, we receive fresh encouragement: "The first step on the road to the Reformation is the recovery of the normal relations of church and state. As soon as one realizes this, there awakens in him the zeal that otherwise slumbers" (p. 119).

Kuyper's attempt to saddle Calvinism with a privatized church and a secular, agnostic state, explains the manifold incongruities and inconsistencies in his system. It would have been bad enough if it were only a system of thought that had to be dealt with. But with Abraham Kuyper, one was dealing not with an armchair theoretician, but with someone who could put his ideas in practice with unparalleled facility. Kuyper was a journalist of the first rank who founded one of the country's leading newspapers, a leading politician capable of imposing the neutral state onto Dutch Christianity, and a churchman who erected a new church from the rubble of the national church which he helped to demolish.

"The gains from this method do not outweigh the losses! We can quickly achieve the immediate goal. But by doing so we lose the church and the people!" (p. 118). For in that case, "The ideal can only be realized through kindred spirits, and for their benefit. And this little group, reduced by the pressure of this principle, is ecclesiastically isolated, while society either becomes more and more secularized or is delivered over to Rome" (p. 118). The result is a Christian ghetto in a hostile society. The short-sightedness of the approach becomes increasingly evident as the decades go by, as Hoedemaker's predictions slowly but surely come to pass.

Certainly, Hoedemaker did not have all the answers. His "An Agenda for Constitutional Reform based on Article 36" (pp. 61ff.) show the signs of the times in which they were written. But the forward-looking nature of Hoedemaker's treatment still shines through, and becomes even more evident when paired with his *Reformed Ecclesiology in an Age of Denominationalism,* to be published as a companion volume to this one. Regardless, the days of naïve faith in neutrality are over. The forces of unbelief are coming into their own, and will stop at nothing to "remove and prevent" the Christian faith and the Christian church from exerting any influence, even from existing, in modern society.[10] There is no evading this state of affairs. The only question is, will we continue to acquiesce in it, or will we – come what may – recognize the failure of accommodation and reassert the lordship of Jesus Christ over every area of life?

---

[10] This was already apparent in Hoedemaker's day: "The modern state does not tolerate the church on its [i.e., the public] terrain. It only knows of [private] clubs, societies, and foundations, and should one desire recognition before the law, it must come in these forms. Speaking of removal, it is not possible to suppress a moral person more effectively than our constitution does" (n. 68, p. 70). It is not a question of whether or not false religion will be "removed and prevented;" the question is, *which* religion will be declared false, and so removed and prevented? In the modern state, it is Christianity which plays the role of false religion, secular humanism the true religion. There is no neutrality in the public square, nor in the schools, nor in academia. There is, rather, a dedicated, ongoing effort to remove and prevent. It is inescapable, and inexorable.

NOTE ON THE TEXT

Hoedemaker could certainly have used a good editor. In places the text is garbled, in others the meaning is unclear, and the line of thought is difficult to follow. As an aid to following the argument, as well as to explain otherwise obscure matters, I have here and there added explanatory interpolations between square brackets. Furthermore, what with the citations being rife with errors, I have made corrections by tracking down nearly all the proper citations.

Square brackets are also used to indicate the word being translated where such a word might be subject to more than one translation, or where more than one original obtains for a certain word, e.g., church (*kerk* or *gemeente*), grace (*genade* or *gratie*). Likewise, titles of works cited are placed in brackets, usually the translation but sometimes the original, where, because of frequency of usage, the translated title is used in the text (e.g., *The Herald, The Standard, Our Program*).

Finally, a word about the word *staatsrecht,* which generally is translated as "constitutional law." I have rendered it literally, as "state law," because 1) it also includes administrative law, and 2) by it, Hoedemaker understands public law generally, together with the law of (private) associations.

"Our Netherland churches also are about to reconsider the article in our Confession which touches on this matter."

Abraham Kuyper, *Lectures on Calvinism,* p. 99.

A PRELIMINARY WORD

The question as to whether a conviction expressed in our Confession is Scriptural puts us on theological ground.

It lies outside the bustle of parties on ecclesiastical and political terrain.

This is an invaluable gain for those who are divided, to the great damage of their spiritual and ecclesiastical lives as well as their labor in the service of the same Lord, who are divided because they did not provide the same response to an entirely different question: how are we to behave and conduct business in the abnormal circumstances to which church and state are subjected in our country?

It would be painful to us if this investigation, which we initiated in the wake of Dr. Kuyper and his articles in *The Herald,* were to be explained in the sense of party spirit.

The same motive power that drove apart what should have remained together *and at bottom remained one,* has falsified the oppositions.

We reject them from the bottom of our hearts and hold fast to our brothers even where they are divided ecclesiastically and have parted ways politically.

Truth unites.

This is demonstrated as soon as *the Confession* is given its due.

To this end, it is not even necessary for one to be in agreement with all and every part of the Confession – if only one is Reformed in this sense, that in the event of deviation from the Confession one appeals to the Word, but then above all cooperates toward the goal lying near at hand, *to put the church in the position to come together for this investigation.*

For at the end of the day, "all the church for all the people" is what really matters.

P. J. Hoedemaker
Amsterdam, April 9th, 1901

ARTICLE 36 OF THE BELGIC CONFESSION

It is generally known that for many who call themselves Reformed, Article 36 of the Belgic Confession is a stumbling block. It is also known that the conviction unambiguously expressed in it deviates to some degree from the principles that the Reformed acting as a political party[11] seek to implement. But beyond this, there is uncertainty regarding the questions stemming from this state of affairs, for a number of reasons.

For instance, to many it is unclear the degree to which the question is simply a matter of semantics, and the degree to which actual principles are involved. And apparently it has never been considered whether this difference, assuming it exists, is of such penetrating nature that it is connected with other deviations of principle.

For those who have no problem adhering to Article 36, this could be enough of a reason to devote a more detailed study to this subject, in order to provide a thought-out rationale.

But there are two objections to this:

1) the subject is not relevant to our times.

2) the questions it involves are not in the least ready to be made a matter of fruitful discussion.

The Relevance of the Theme

Regarding 1), how can anyone say that this subject is not relevant? Have we forgotten that since the days of Groen van Prinsterer there has been a great deal of movement in the area of politics?

On the contrary: Alongside the existing political parties there is certainly a place for a party that finds its reason for being in Article 36 of the Belgic

---

[11] [i.e., the Anti-Revolutionary Party.]

Confession, i.e., for a party that derives its principles, its program, its motivations and motives from that article, misunderstood by many, rejected by others, and neglected by all.

In that case, there would no longer be a reason to say that the subject is not relevant. Everyone active in politics or interested in it would then have to acquaint themselves with the pros and cons of this standpoint.

Yet when it only concerns the question, what does the Confession say, and what does Holy Scripture teach, we can interest no one, at least among the public at large, in a treatment pertaining as it does to the dogmatic-exegetical field, because we then stand entirely outside the practical world. What does it matter whether we know how to understand the words, "remove and prevent all idolatry and false religion"? What does it profit us if we demonstrate that civil government is to promote the kingdom of Christ and the preaching of the gospel, and to cast down the kingdom of the Antichrist?

No – actually, we take this back. It certainly would matter. An argument about how to understand Article 36, which when applied has certain consequences for the practice of the state, does mean something. Every principled explanation of things must sooner or later have a powerful effect and so prove to be tremendously practical.

Nevertheless, for those whose study and sympathy lie in an entirely different area, this is not enough motivation for them to occupy themselves with this particular subject, under the current circumstances.

Are the Times Ripe?

Regarding 2) as to whether the questions are ripe for discussion: It is not a question of comparing an article from a confession with a political program. These represent two very distinct stages in the development of the truth. In order to obtain a proper discussion and not be exposed to all kinds of fallacies, one must compare confession with confession, principles with principles, and system with system.

In the development and explanation of the truth, namely, there are always these three stages:

1) In its confession, the church summarizes, as if in a focal point, what is taught regarding various matters in Holy Scripture.

2) From that confession the principles are derived that make it fruitful for life and foster its dominion in every area of life, not least in scientific research.

3) According to and along with these principles, there is, as the case may be, the formation of theory, the enactment of a program, the erection of a system.

If a religious conviction is compared with a system that is the fruit of much reflection and much research, then we easily get confused and we allow all sorts of wrong conclusions. For example, we come to remarkable conclusions like the following: "The civil government which best promotes the kingdom of Christ does not allow itself to get involved in that kingdom. The truly neutral government thus acts most in accordance with our Confession."

In such cases it is undoubtedly quite useful to expose the fallacy in the argument, but this is a thankless task when done for the benefit of those who have no interest in being corrected on this point. He who seeks to bring the men of the third stage back to the first, or in other words, from their own conceptions back to Scripture, becomes for them, by their very nature, someone standing in their way. If he places the statements of faith against a system born from the need of the moment and from the requirements of practice, he encounters new difficulties at every step, first in the area of intentions, then in that of exegesis, and finally that of practice, where the principle of utility holds sway.

What, pray tell, is the fatal defect that hinders so many who call themselves Reformed from finding in Article 36 of the Belgic Confession of Faith the expression of their conviction? Not the result of new insights into the truth, nor the consequence of some special conception of certain texts or parts of Holy Scripture; in a word, not the result of the ongoing investigation of Scripture; but exclusively causes which lie in the times, and in apostasy from the living God. It is so easy to ask mainly or exclusively how this or that objection can be removed as soon as possible, and in the most advantageous manner. But what before all things should have been asked and, if possible, determined, is what God teaches regarding His Word, and to assess the systems, the principles, the insights of men by the touchstone of the Word of God alone.

Now, though, when the opportunity has unexpectedly come up to test by Holy Scripture the basic principles by which a movement acts in the political arena,[12] these two objections to a more deliberate examination of Article 36 in connection with the deviating opinions of those who call themselves Reformed and, as such, act as leaders in the political field, fall away.

The as-yet unmentioned objection also falls away, that those who are happy to agree with the aforementioned article do not yet have to consider themselves competent, and certainly ought not yet feel called, to transition from theological to political terrain.

We do not have to be experts or scholars to consult the Bible and confess the truth. What is more, in the case in point, we cannot and should not withdraw from the investigation. In the first place, out of respect for those to whom we have referred above as "those who call themselves Reformed," so as to leave entirely to one side whether they call themselves this rightly or wrongly, rather than announce ahead of time that they mistakenly do so.

Unfaithful confessors there have been at all times; the Remonstrants in the 17th century also called themselves Reformed; builders using wood, hay, and stubble to erect a building on the true foundation, are unfortunately not rare. But among those who reject Article 36 are in the first place the men who set themselves the task of leading our people back to the paths entered by the fathers, the paths of the Word from which the children have wandered. And to a certain degree, they have actually succeeded in this. Many of them are members of churches which were born from reaction to the doctrinal liberalism existing in the national church. They are leaders of public opinion who are very well aware that the purity of scientific investigation and its results cannot be safeguarded unless one has the ability to check the principles derived from the Confession, for which reason they have set a "guard over the principle."[13]

---

[12] [A reference to the series of articles on church and state in *The Herald.* See the appendix.]

[13] ["De wacht bij het beginsel": A reference to an article in *The Herald* by Kuyper, which became a slogan for proponents of Reformed orthodoxy. For further details, see Kuipers, *Abraham Kuyper: An Annotated Bibliography 1857–2010*, p. 275.]

A Question of Semantics?

There is only one consideration that would prevent us from carrying out a further investigation on this point: the idea that this is a question of semantics. However, there is no ground for this idea. The Separated Reformed church has already removed everything that is objectionable in Article 36, to the extent that this could be done by simple editing.

Their synodal decisions contain the following on this point: "After being asked for a clear statement of the meaning of Article 36 of our Confession of Faith, and the purpose of that question explained by the deputies of North Holland and Utrecht, the article itself was first read for that purpose. The assembly judges that the purpose of this article is, that it is fitting for the civil government as such that it, as God's servant, protect the true doctrine and religion, and with the power given it by God, remove all false religions and idolatries by such means as it judges to be right and fair according to God's Word."[14]

Furthermore, in 1861, under the influence of the United Scottish Church, which, as is known, was born out of opposition to the state church and therefore is greatly estranged from the mind of our fathers regarding the political sphere, it expressly stated that secular power has nothing to say in or about the church. But the following was added immediately afterward:

"However, by this we do not say that the civil government should have no influence whatsoever regarding the church; on the contrary, we desire that the government protect the church, and that it exert its influence everywhere to ward off evil and promote that which is wholesome, according to Article 36 of our Confession. But we do not ascribe to it any ruling power or authority in or

---

[14] *Handelingen van de Synode der Christelijk Afgescheidene Gereformeerde Kerk in Nederland Leiden 1857* [Acts of the Synod of the Christian Separated Reformed Church in the Netherlands, Leyden 1857] (Kampen: S. van Velzen Jr., 1857), Article 160, pp. 73–74.

about the church, for the Lord is our judge, the Lord is our lawgiver, the Lord is our king."[15]

The Systemic Consequence of Deviation

There is indeed a question of a deviation from the Confession, which runs very deep in the life of the church and is pressed by all sorts of objections.

In the first place, by an objection of a church-legal nature. The right to appeal against one article includes the same right with regard to other articles. The Moderns were able to hide their ecclesiastical position behind the opposition of the Nonconformists [Gereformeerden] to Article 36.

This objection is all the more pressing because the deviation from the Confession results in a deviation in the science connected with it. Article 36 contains the architectonic principle according to which a corresponding system of civil punishment, and any other right, must be set up.

But deviation from this article posits a similar principle in addition to and opposed to it. Those whom we have in mind here are the first to point out this connection. Hence the false position by which men whose church-legal position in ordinary circumstances would be that of defendants, instead are able to act as reformers who are able to punish the deviations of others with exile from the patrimonial estate. We are exposed to this by the peculiar condition of church and state among us, the disorganization, the unrest, the party system – direct and indirect consequences of the apostasy into which our people sink ever deeper. The moment is so well suited for anybody to impose a private opinion on the church, and to use the obvious means to that end to gain power in the hope of spreading the blessing along the way – the blessing which everyone expects to realize from the application of his own principles and the implementation of his own ideas.

---

[15] *Kerkelijk handboekje opnieuw uitgegeven door de Synode der Afgescheiden Gereformeerde Gemeente gehouden te Hoogeveen 1861* [Ecclesiastical Manual Reissued by the Synod of the Separated Reformed Church held in Hoogeveen 1861] (Kampen: G. Ph. Zalsman, 1861), n.p.

If it is from the Confession that the principles are derived which determine the source, the material, and the direction of a science, any deviation from the Confession must, as has already been pointed out, become visible in the science under its influence. It follows again that, under the existing circumstances, church and state in particular and, more specifically, dogmatics as well as church law and state law, get more or less reconstructed under this influence.

One Confession with Separatism?

This was already seen and remarked upon prior to the Nonconformity, in a public lecture at the start of the school year at the Free University in Amsterdam, in response to attempts to give this school and the education it provides a non-ecclesiastical character. "Reformed," it was then called. [16] Reformed is Re-formed, i.e., "Christian" purified of errors. So it was said that we should hold all the purified churches that departed from Rome, including the Lutheran, to be (more or less) Reformed, i.e., sister churches, and because of this could not regard the university as only a nursery for the Reformed church.

Rightly so, when nothing more and nothing other than this is intended. But something else was intended. The intention was that the Free University, or rather the Association for Higher Education, would not take sides in the question between us and the Separated Reformed. In my view this is a fatal error which did not bring the least advantage to our university and could bring about its demise.

It is necessary to state this unreservedly, that eyes might be opened to it. The union of all the Reformed in the entire country – who would not want that with all their heart? But is it Reformed in the sense given above that is intended? No. It is rather the Separated Reformed, whose confession – so they say – is our confession. Is this so? That the Separated Reformed church in many respects stands closer to us than any other sister church is something that no one will

---

[16] P. J. Hoedemaker, *Op het fondament der apostelen en profeten* [On the Foundation of the Apostles and Prophets], (Utrecht: C. van Bentum, 1886), pp. 211–218. [The lecturer was Hoedemaker, and the lecture was "Waarom studeert gij nog theologie aan de vrije universiteit?" (Why study theology at the Free University?), pp. 194–223.]

dispute. But does the question that separates us stand outside the Confession, dogmatics, theology? This is the implicit assumption of e.g. the Reformed Ministers' Conference, and because it is, I have, since the meeting in "De Vrede" in Amsterdam[17] at which a proposal intended to affirm this difference was rejected, stopped attending, just as I have no intention to attend until there is a prospect of a pure position in this matter.

The basic error, in my view, lies in the thesis: "We are agreed in the Confession, but not in the practice of church life." We are *not* agreed in the Confession, and I fear that we will never be so unless it pleases God in His grace to restore our historic and true (not "older"), albeit wretched Reformed church.

The difference lies mainly in the articles regarding the church and the relation of church and state. No synod has yet ascertained that difference. It has not been brought to general awareness. But it lies in the heart and experience of a large portion of the people of the Lord in this country, those who have resisted the temptation to separate, not out of ancillary intentions or conservatism, but from a right theological instinct, and have spoken with deeds: we are not going to Ulrum![18] Let me add: it is implicitly contained in the Forms of Unity, like the content of the Counter-Remonstrance of 1611 was implicitly contained therein.

I am not forgetting that there are two elements in the Separated Reformed church, although the union chartered by this designation was established some

---

[17] [No further specifics. This could be a reference to the conference of July 1884, at which Kuyper expressed great interest in joining forces with the Separated Reformed. Prof. Herman Bavinck, who taught at the seminary of the Separated Reformed in Kampen, was chosen as presiding officer (moderamen) of the conference. See further, *Acta van het Synodaal Convent (1887) en van de voorlopige synoden van de Nederduitsche Gereformeerde Kerken (1888–1892)* [Acts of the Synodal Convent and the provisional synods of the Dutch Reformed churches] (Kampen: J. H. Kok, 1985), pp. 20–21.]

[18] [A reference to the separation which began in Ulrum under the leadership of Rev. Hendrik de Cock in 1834, which led to the formation of the Separated Reformed church.]

years ago.[19] I also realize full well that one can be "national Reformed" and still stand foursquare in the "the separation." But as long as this principle is not defeated in terms of principle, that is, on theological grounds, I do not consider the future of the Free University to be secure.

The Marnix Society,[20] the attempt to establish a gymnasium [college preparatory school] and many more things are misunderstood as long as they are only seen as "churchism," i.e., unnecessary, personal matters and not matters of principle, a principle weightier than goodwill, spiritual sympathies, and brotherly well-wishes. From this list, we can learn that the Reformed principle upon which we founded our university is not neutral territory between us and "the separation" but the area that we have wrested from it.

One Confession with Nonconformity?

In his *Joint Witness regarding the church incident in Amsterdam*,[21] Prof. J. H. Gunning held every Reformed person responsible for that which Dr. Kuyper and his followers sought in the name of their confession. I, however, rejected this joint responsibility.

My response:

> Although this letter is more specifically intended to give you thanks for sending me your 'Joint Witness,' and I only wish to add a few remarks which will provide you with proof that I have tried to follow your train of thought, I consider both your assumption and your conclusion so questionable, so damaging to fraternity, that you will surely wish to afford me the opportunity to inform you why I must decisively reject the one and the other.

---

[19] [To wit, an Independentistic element and an element which looked forward to reunion with the national church, when the latter will have been purified.]

[20] [An association founded in 1868 by Kuyper and others to sponsor publication of research into the Reformed church in the Netherlands in the 16th century. See Jasper Vree, *The Marnix-Vereeniging: Abraham Kuyper's First National Organisation (1868-89)*, in *Nederlands archief voor kerkgeschiedenis / Dutch Review of Church History*, Vol. 84 (2004), pp. 388-475.]

[21] *Mede-getuigenis in zake het kerkelijk incident te Amsterdam* ('s-Gravenhage: Beschoor, 1886).

Let me then say to you that as a member of a church the confession of which I am in heartfelt agreement, I am not disposed to allow myself to be lumped into a 'party.'

If it is true, as you say, that Dr. Kuyper acted as party head in our church, I think I can demand of him that he conform to me, rather than that I conform to him.

After all, he has not kept secret that his view of the vocation of civil government, at least in one point, deviates from that which is taught in our Confession in Article 36.

Now I am not disputing that either he or anyone else has the right to claim, and if possible to show, that God's Word teaches something else than what the church has hitherto thought that it said. The Holy Spirit can tell "new things" to the children of our age from this treasure; but sufficient authority cannot be attributed either to this claim nor to anything else associated with it, for it may turn out that the entire Confession forms one unbreakable whole in all its parts, so that one deviation, considered in its extreme consequences, contains all other deviations.

I do not hesitate to acknowledge what God in Dr. Kuyper has meant to our church, and am fully prepared to bear the reproach borne by him for the principle of that church. I do not even wish to detract from this what more specifically might be attributable to the man, the sinner, the editor, the spokesman; I do not think that I, as you, in my view, very wrongly demand of me, have to stand against everything I find mistaken in Dr. Kuyper's action, which is to say, all that I might have said and done differently (except only to the extent that the church, which I love, is threatened by it). Regardless of all this, I do not wish to be held personally liable by you or anyone else for something that does not directly stem from the concept of the church, or spontaneously from collegial relationship and the bond of friendship, in accordance with general principles of law and morality.

As a member of the church, wholeheartedly committed to its Confession, I am released from the snares of 'the coterie' and 'the party,' and I am not disposed, simply because I am Reformed, or because in practice I adhere to what I consider to be a sound conception of academic science, to have a yoke imposed upon myself.[22]

I later spoke in the same spirit to those, not on the *outside,* but on the *inside.* As a protest against the means by which it was sought to purify the national Reformed church of modernism.

We consider it impermissible to organize ecclesiastically, officially or unofficially, a certain group of members and pastors, or to make of our deeply sunken local church, which more or less reflects the condition of the church in its entirety, a Reformed [Gereformeerde] church, which, under the circumstances, would be to make it a Separated church, by, e.g., signing the Three Forms of Unity while neither standing nor wishing to stand on our own, nor still practicing ecclesial communion with other churches.

In this way, the best we will achieve will be the separation of a certain part of the national church which consciously accepts the Reformed Confession, while leaving the other part behind, which should not have been relinquished. Is this what we want? *I* do not.

And furthermore:

We wholeheartedly endorse the Three Forms of Unity, but we also recognize the right of appeal to God's Word.

Well then, as long as our church has no form in which a national synod is possible, which means that the tacit condition for signing the Three Forms is not fulfilled, we oppose, for the sake of the brothers and churches who think they have gravamina, every premature anticipation of an ideal that is not entirely inaccessible by following the right path.[23]

And at the end of this essay, the following prophecy was made which, alas! speedily found fulfillment:

---

[22] Hoedemaker, *Op het Fondament,* pp. 439–441.

[23] *Ibid.,* pp. 153–154.

There is certainly a way out: along the lines of the Separated Reformed. After all, nothing as completely removes the possibility of a reorganization, as was recommended in the synod's assembly last year, as the pleasant prospect, which would give the Moderns the greatest pleasure, of the extreme right wing being rendered harmless by the power of its principle.

Thus, in the end, the only possible solution of the issues may lie in the direction taken by the leadership. But who will prove that this was, or should be, the only possible one, that it is the most desirable one, and that it is the most favorable one to church and fatherland?[24]

When, therefore, the move to Nonconformity had come, and the Free University no longer served its original purpose, when at least those who loved and continued to love the national Reformed church for what it was in its actual essence and could be in its manifestation no longer were able to function as curators, directors or professors without renouncing their principle, and the outgoing rector[25] actually denied in his oration (in the opinion of one of the Nonconformists) that there was a principled reason for leaving the university, the following was written [by Hoedemaker], under the impression of what he there and then heard.

The Three Forms of Unity are accepted by you and your kindred spirits, as is known, with one exception. With regard to the duty of the civil government as described in Article 36 of our Confession, you think that God's Word gives you freedom to depart from the fairly unanimous opinion of the fathers. The exception is seemingly so insignificant, that in your eye it must have something of petty banter to be reminded of it.

And yet I must do so in order to reveal the deeper ground of our difference.

It lies in your deviation on this one point from the Confession and the practice of the fathers.

---

[24] *Ibid.*, p. 156.

[25] [A reference to A. F. de Savornin Lohman, to whom the following epistle was directed.]

When this question is belittled, it is reduced to the question as to whether the civil government is called to apply the sword to heretics. This immediately gets public opinion, including among the Reformed, on one's side.

But we should not fixate on a few expressions.

After all, doctrines are similar to geological layers. At a certain place, a bit of underlying granite sticks out which has broken through later formations by the effect of volcanic powers. But even where we do not see granite, it is still present deep below the calcium and sandstone.

Here is another image. An inconspicuous and entirely isolated deviation from the Confession is like the results of the books, when the balance sheet is drawn up. There is an almost entirely insignificant difference. But that difference causes headaches. The accountant has to run through everything again and recalculate, because that slight deviation might conceal a much larger irregularity.

When I run through your argument of this afternoon, in which, need I say it? there is very much with which I wholeheartedly agree while also providing me a literary delight, it shows that you yourself have fully felt the strength of the principle that you have advocated.

However, I felt even more; I felt how much was involved in that deviation. There lies the principle that, within the mass of convictions, is connected with the question at which our ways part. The issues, namely, that concern the church, church government, the Reformation, the university and its neutrality.

This was the thing that moved me when you said: 'Professor Hoedemaker has applied for dismissal; fortunately not because he disagrees with the basis of our foundation'!

You spoke correctly.

But that is precisely why, once again, I must ask this question from the heart, and only for the sake of truth: Do you and I have the same right to invoke this basis? Just as much right to claim that we are faithful to the Confession of our church, which both you and I have ratified with our signatures?

I only ascertain that between you and me lies a difference.

In confession.

A difference that, thought through, has led to the rupture between us in the area of the church and in that of the school.

I do not think to dispute your right to test the Confession against the Word at the points in question, and subject it to a closer investigation using all the tools which experience, history, and science provide, and if necessary, without prejudice to the right of the church, to maintain it, even to contradict it.

It is precisely for this reason that I wholeheartedly reject the principle of your so-called Reformation etc., and your appeal to the Three Forms of Unity, in connection with the local church or the churches which, under this erroneous and misleading principle, were later brought together under an apparently Reformed church government.

Here lies the deeper-seated difference.

For I assert that you are guilty of an immense *hysteron proteron* [a reversal of the proper order] in the interest of your Free Church; the church, not of our Reformed fathers, but adapted to the times of Vinet, De Labadie, and Schleiermacher, when you made use of the abnormal situation to separate church and school from each other, the better to separate church and state, theology and political science, from each other.

It did not have to happen like this.

It took place under cover of a false principle – neutrality, as described above.

And that principle makes me receive the testimony coming from you, for which I humbly thank you: 'Professor Hoedemaker has applied for dismissal; fortunately not because he disagrees with the principle upon which our university and association are based.'

Not we, perhaps, but the representatives of the principles that you and I confess, will discuss this, when we are at rest, in twenty, fifty, a hundred years, if the struggle lasts that long, whether or not they remember what you said![26]

In these quotations from essays and periodicals dating from the time before, during, and after the schism, it was thus expressed in an unambiguous manner that the Nonconformity and everything connected with it either led to this end,

---

[26] *Ééne Belijdenis? Eene ernstige vraag naar aanleiding van mijn aftreden als Hoogleeraar aan de Vrije Universiteit* [One and the Same Confession? A serious question prompted by my resignation as professor at the Free University] (Amsterdam: J. H. Kruyt, 1887), pp. 8–9, 28–29.

or was directly or indirectly a result of it, or at least was inseparable from the deviations *which had yet to be ecclesiastically examined*, with which not a few calling themselves Reformed ought to be charged.

The question is not yet whether what is claimed here can also be proved. This proof can only be provided when an opportunity is given to lay out the propositions, in particular concerning church and state, that are concerned here, and to show how these propositions and related issues are connected with the question of the vocation of civil government. For the time being, the primary concern is with the great importance of dogmatic investigation into the right of objections to Article 36; secondly, the sufficient cause for this writer to participate in that investigation; and thirdly, the correct understanding of the nature and significance of this investigation, which, without any doubt, should have *preceded* the formation of an anti-revolutionary party.

Let us leave to one side whether those who have already proceeded to the dogmatic, ecclesiastical, church-legal and scientific application of not yet legitimized deviations from Article 36, especially in the area of constitutionalism and politics, are the appropriate and morally competent men to initiate the investigation in question. Let us even assume that it will be possible for them, even now, to test and correct the deviation, the related political system, and the resulting schism in the church, against Holy Scripture. In any case, it is certain that the investigation in question is indeed about the existence of the Anti-Revolutionary Party and of the church formations outside the national Reformed church. What is at issue, in fact, is their right to regard themselves, from the moral point of view, as the legitimate heirs of the Reformed fathers, and to bear the name "Reformed" strictly speaking.

We will return to this in a postscript,[27] because it has no direct bearing on the treatment of the objections against Article 36. Allow us to note in passing that the assertion which we, lastly, hope to establish in detail, was not the monotone refrain of unmotivated complaints (as appears from the above-mentioned quotations, which could be multiplied indefinitely), but is repeated in different contexts.

---

[27] [presumably ch. 3, "The State with the Bible."]

It was pronounced the first time as a result of the attempts to downplay the ecclesiastical and church-legal variance between the Separated church and the national church.

It was voiced the second time when Prof. Gunning expressed the accusation, which he has not yet withdrawn, that those who did not follow Kuyper in everything had to be judged, not according to their words, but according to their deeds, since anyone who called himself "Reformed" ["Gereformeerd"] or was in the service of the Association for Higher Education on the Reformed Basis, had the moral obligation to accept unconditionally the party, the party head, and party policy!

It also put an answer on the lips of the outgoing professor [i.e., Hoedemaker], at the annual meeting of the Free University when he heard, not a farewell salute, nor a declaration of regret, nor any remark on how unfortunate it was that a difference of insight had come to disrupt the harmony in this circle, but rather the cynical remark which forced him to express the conviction, reaffirmed by the hearing of principles contrary to the Confession: "It is precisely because we disagree in the Confession that what was once joined together by the Confession is now separated by it!" That was the third time it was expressed.

The text from which the just-cited quotation was taken[28] ends with an appeal to the future. Not as a result of the desire, in the end, to be shown right. Alas, this reaffirmation of an opinion expressed in 1886 cannot revoke the history of the last fifteen years. Rather, as an expression of the firm belief that the truth must sooner or later become manifest.

Sooner than one could anticipate at the time, it seems to be manifesting itself. But whether this is more than just appearance will only become clear over time.

The Long-Awaited Attempt to Justify the Deviation from Article 36

But enough of this.

Efforts are now being made on the part of the dissenters to arrive, if possible, at a revision of Article 36. There is therefore reason for us, not in the first place

---

[28] See n. 26.

to come back to the related issues – this will, as has been said, be done in a postscript – but to put the objections brought against Article 36 to the test and thereby participate in the investigation to be instituted.

When the first step in this direction was taken in 1896, we greeted this as a hopeful first step. We read the following in the September 10th, 1896 issue of *The Reformed Church*,[29] under the title, "AN IMPORTANT ANNOUNCE-MENT," taken from the daily report of the Nonconformist Synod, regarding Article 36 of the Confession:

> To the General Synod of the Reformed Churches in the Netherlands.
>
> With all the members of the Synod who were summoned by the chairman on the 11th of August to assent to the Forms of Unity of the Churches by standing up at their seats, the undersigned also responded to this summons without expressly mentioning their gravamen against a clause in Article 36 of the Confession. They abstained from assenting, since they could not otherwise suppose that their gravamen was sufficiently known to their fellow members. Now however (also rightly in their judgment) that the existence of dormant gravamina has been rejected by the Synod as being dangerous to the purity of doctrine and therefore the welfare of the churches, they have decided they cannot leave the Synod without tendering this objection to the content and the tenor of the 3rd clause in Article 36 of the Confession of Churches, as not conforming to the Word of God.
>
> They proceed from the, in their view, indisputable truth, that we, confessing the Confession of our fathers, may not understand by the words in which our fathers confess, anything other than what they themselves, according to the definite testimony of history, intended with the use of these words; and that thus understood and conceived, this 3rd clause of Article 36 of our Confession, in sincere and honest interpretation, among other things obligates the secular government to remove idolatry and false religion if necessary with the sword, and makes it incumbent upon the Churches to preach this to the civil government as its duty. Considering this to be contrary to the Word of God, they are obliged

---

[29] [*De Gereformeerde Kerk,* the weekly newspaper founded and initially edited by Hoedemaker.]

in their conscience not to confess this statement, but to reject it, and, they, subject to this, put their declaration in this matter in the hands of the Churches, invoking the Churches' judgment on this matter, prepared at all times to stand firm in their declaration on the basis of Holy Scripture.

F. L. Rutgers, M. Noordtzij, D. Wielenga, L. Lindeboom, P. Biesterveld, A. Kuyper, H. Bavinck, J. H. Donner.

Middelburg, September 4th, 1896.

The Synod appointed Rev. T. Bos, A. Littooy, Prof. H. Bavinck, Prof. A. Kuyper, T. Heemskerk LL. M., Dr. D. P. D. Fabius, Tromp of Rotterdam, and Wind of Haren, to provide an opinion regarding this gravamen to the next Synod, which is to be sent to the churches a year ahead of time. The views of the foreign Reformed churches should also be made known in this matter as appropriate.

This announcement is remarkable in many respects.

1) For the first time it was *officially* ascertained that a significant deviation from the doctrine of the Reformed church is found in the [Nonconformist] Reformed Churches.

2) Also, that such deviations will no longer be tolerated there.

3) In consequence, it is now stated that the 3rd clause of Article 36, which commands the civil government to maintain the honor of God in *its legal sphere*, i.e., in the terrain of public life, with its coercive power, and to remove all idolatry and blasphemy, *does not agree with God's Word*.

The confessors of the truth, in particular the Reformed in the national church, must therefore take up for the Confession on this point, as long as that which is asserted by the leading men of the assembly in Middelburg *is not conclusively demonstrated*.

In the Synod's daily report, from which the above message was taken, the decision by the nonconformists to have made known "as appropriate" the view in this matter of the foreign churches was also announced. So did the editors think and speak in 1896. The hint by *The Reformed Church* that this would be easier said than done, is not very important in this regard, because it refers to a matter of a church-legal nature which is unimportant to us.

Enough. We have set our sights on a response to the question regarding the right of Article 36. But we are writing in 1900, not 1896. Patience has been tried for long enough. There was even reason to fear that the entire matter had been forgotten. Happily, that is not the case. We hear nothing of the Commission appointed in 1896. But *The Herald* [30] is now busy coming up with the evidence that the fathers made a mistake regarding the vocation of civil government. [31] Not only has the gravamen in question had time to summer and to winter, but one can also say that the discourse in which the evidence is being provided to us, has been worked out quite broadly. These matters are not being treated in *The Herald* in a passing fashion.

The Need for a Theological Basis for Political Science

As we wait for the completion of the argument, we will take the liberty in this "foreword" to highlight the significance of this labor in *The Herald* by way of an illustrative example.

One of the speakers at the "extraordinary classical assembly" recently held in Amsterdam declared that he could not understand how somebody could say, regarding discussions during such assemblies, that matters were dealt with apart from God's Word. After all, everyone is free to make an appeal to God's Word!

According to that point of view, it is entirely superfluous, whether in the field of science or of practice, to take into account the truth enshrined in the common Confession and the principles to be derived from it as the point of departure; one only needs to defend his opinion by an appeal to some verse of Scripture.

It is therefore not superfluous to make clear by an example how much we owe Dr. Kuyper for the work he is currently undertaking to show what can be deduced from Holy Scripture regarding the points associated with the important declaration made at the assembly in Middelburg.

---

[30] [*De Heraut,* the weekly church-oriented newspaper edited by Kuyper.]

[31] [A reference to the series of articles by Kuyper on church and state. See the appendix.]

That work was and still is necessary. There is no other way to escape the nameless confusion in which one is caught in so many, but especially ecclesiastical-political, areas.

There is also no other means to bring together what belongs together. Why is that?

Allow me to say just this. Over and over, every possible issue is reasoned to death without ever succeeding in coming to a successful conclusion or convincing the opposing party. Why? Because we do not first ascertain what Scripture says on the point in question. Theology has ceased to be the queen of the sciences, what's more, the guide to truth. This is the origin of so much unprincipledness and uncertainty. In this way, every discussion becomes a game of wit, and the evidence before which one momentarily yields gives the impression that one could just as well have proved the opposite. Whether or not one appeals to Holy Scripture is irrelevant. It is not hard to insert one's own opinion, or that of the party to which one counts oneself, into Scripture.

A proponent of women's right to vote recently asked in the classical assembly whether Mary had not chosen the good part when she sat down at Jesus' feet, while Martha busied herself with outward things, and thought to have proved by this that women should be given a share in the government of the church. After all, according to him that is what it means to sit at the feet of Jesus! This is evidence of the need to establish what one can, ought, and would like to demonstrate from Scripture, before appealing to it.

This is also true of politics. Theology has a certain kind of work to do, before the political party leader may speak. It must establish what Dr. Kuyper, assuming he is correct, is busy setting forth in *The Herald* regarding the vocation of the civil government, among other things. Otherwise, the various interests, notions, systems, pass each other in opposite directions, like trains of different companies leaving the same station, each on different tracks. There can be no arriving at an answer as to who is right and who is wrong.

There is a difference in policy regarding politics. It is rooted, as stated above, according to our most inward conviction, *in the difference in confession*. But this can first be demonstrated when our starting point is not abnormal reality, but the Confession, and Holy Scripture as summarized in the Confession.

We take as an example the ten articles Dr. Kuyper published in *The Standard*[32] at roughly the same time that the articles on church and state appeared in *The Herald,* by way of kicking off the impending political campaign.[33] Beginning January 31st, 1900, the articles concerned the contradistinction, "Protestant or Christian."

We summarize this argument in the form of a few statements drawn from it, with a few scattered notes on our part, as proof that such arguments, no matter how much of the beautiful and the true they contain, for all kinds of reasons do not prove anything, and consequently do not convince.

The Standard reasons as follows: Those who confess Christ constitute the great majority both among and outside the voters. Our political situation directly contradicts this. Hence the question: Whether the rallying together of Christian groups could be brought about to eliminate the inequality.

We already start to lose sight of the issue. Is the majority then sovereign? Is the majority right? Is the majority the strongest? Is this the teaching of Holy Scripture? Is this the experience of the church? We tread the well-worn path.

The Scriptures have nothing to do with this. The starting point of this line of reasoning is abnormal reality. The Revolution has shifted the origin and the center of gravity of all power and authority. We now live under the rule of the principle: the most votes win! People no longer ask: What is right? What is true? What is God's will? What does Scripture say? The issue everywhere in the world is simply this: if you are in the minority, you will be squeezed to death. Would you like to continue to compete in the area of the church, of the school, with respect to various Christian, social, private interests, with the negative or positive help of the neutral government, by virtue of the principle "equal rights for all," then do your best to become a majority in a given moment, by coalition, in consequence of the constantly interrupted balance of parties, thanks to a prudent party policy in which we understand the art of fomenting the activity of friends by appealing to their own interests, and exploiting the cleverness of opponents or defusing their opposition in the same way!

---

[32] [*De Standaard,* the daily politics/current events-oriented newspaper edited by Kuyper.]

[33] [As a result of which Kuyper would become Prime Minister.]

The advantages of this system are many. It gets immediate results. Many hope or suspect that in the end the interests of the kingdom of God will be promoted by it. But – and this is the only thing that matters to us in this context – if one were to take Scripture as starting point, one could not apply it; it would not even occur to him, for an obvious reason.

If one proceeds from Scripture, one is faced with questions about the origin of authority, the extent of the task of government, the nature of its office, the rule of its actions. And on these points the churches, and the orientations derived from the application of the principles which they derive from their divergent creeds in the area of the state, diverge so much that there can be no coalition between them.

The differences are too great, too far-reaching; they are too closely associated with all kinds of ecclesiastical or anti-ecclesiastical interests.

And ... the rallying together which is spoken of here will consist in forgetting these differences? Substantial differences! Differences inseparable from real or perceived self-interest! Is that going to work? Is that the lesson of experience in, for example, ecclesiastical matters? There the righteous stand as individuals against tens and hundreds! The argument of *The Standard* would fit exactly into a brochure of one of the modernist church electoral colleges.[34] Could not the people be better motivated by reference to a purely national principle, corresponding to the Confession of the Reformed church? What should we say when the people ask us whether this "rallying together" ends up benefiting Rome and fostering the fragmentation of the church? But there is no end to the questions here.

We read on. Will the "rallying together" be "Protestant" or "Christian"? Is there not even another opposition here, "Calvinistic" or "not Calvinistic"? But we can leave that to one side for the time being.

We again start to lose sight of the issue. Is there a *choice* here? Is the Protestant not a Christian, and the Calvinist not a Protestant? Does the

---

[34] [Electoral colleges ("kiesverenigingen") were groups of church members with voting rights, entitled to select elders and deacons, and to call pastors. In areas with larger populations, these electoral colleges were sizeable and would publish their own materials, such as brochures, in favor of candidates and policies.]

difference between these three not lie in the fact that the Protestant draws the circle in which he seeks cooperation somewhat smaller than he who wants to include everything that is called Christian; and that he who calls himself "Calvinist" draws the circle even more narrowly?

But here again we tread the well-worn path. The quotation above is directly related to what follows, which, however, cannot be understood unless one considers an ambiguity hidden in the above expressions. Which is why we have offered this explanation first. Words like "Christian" can be taken either in the sense indicated by the use of language, or in the sense established by history, or, in agreement with the latter, in the true sense, the sense corresponding to reality. If only the meaning of the words is established in advance by mutual agreement, this cannot do much harm. But without prior definition, there is every reason to play and juggle with concepts. If, based on the usage of speech, the concept of Protestantism is made as vague and the notion of Christianity is made as positive as possible, while the concept "Calvinist" is kept out of the series, then with a little skill, one will be able to draw any conclusion that one desires. In the argument of *The Standard*, only the name Protestant is described.

The contrast is thus indicated in the following way:

"Protestant" is a name for what in principle turns against the Roman hierarchy. In no single circle of significance is there any sign of weakening that contrast. Politically, Protestantism, unlike Rome, demands "freedom of conscience." But in practice, this difference falls away because:

1) The Romanists are in the minority.
2) They have the highest interest in freedom of conscience.
3) They have never committed an attack on this freedom here.

We no longer lose sight of the issue. A detailed argument would be required to examine the various assumptions underlying this reasoning. Obviously, this will not do: few would be interested in reading such pernickety work, even if someone could be found who was interested with enough time on his hands for it.

By way of example: *Is* "Protestant" a name that, in the sense here intended, only opposes the hierarchy? Does Protestantism, for example, have nothing to do with the pretension of Popery's supremacy, with the doctrine of infallibility, with that of the church in connection with the interpretation of Scripture, etc.,

etc.? Is non-Roman Christianity not opposed in principle to Rome, beyond the exception specified by the writer?

There are twenty or more symptoms which make it clear that the opposition indicated here has indeed weakened; the article from which we now cite a few things, indeed the entire view of Dr. Kuyper proves it.

And what about the peculiar restriction in the final paragraph of *The Standard's* argument? It is simply untrue that the opposition is concentrated in the question of freedom of conscience. Article 29 of the Belgic Confession teaches us something else.

From this we can see very clearly the necessity of the theological investigation initiated by *The Herald*.

The Standard's argument can be explained in the following way. People wish to have seats in the parliament, preferably in the government, and believe that this will be in the interests of the Christian school and the Christian church. But if this is to happen, it has to happen at the ballot box, in the usual manner. Hence this plea.

The opposition between Roman and Protestant only lies where *The Standard* seeks it? I thought that Rome had a supreme head who appoints and dismisses kings, and tells them what they should teach and should believe. I thought that according to Rome marriage was a sacrament, so that a Protestant, strictly speaking, is not legitimately married but lives in fornication. But I won't go any further. The opposition is intentionally taken by *The Standard* in such a way that the question as to whether our state will or will not be constituted in the Roman fashion is left unsaid.

Again, this argument clearly shows the necessity of the investigation undertaken by *The Herald*.

The Standard does not ask: What does the Word say; but, how are things in reality? It reasons in this way: "The most votes win. It will be of little use to us to argue about whether this is right or wrong. Where many people wrestle for power, and to achieve something or other which they deem desirable, the only question for us is: whether we will allow the opportunity to slip away to gain some advantage in the interest of the good cause? This system has worked wrongly. Granted. But this does not detract from the fact that we also have to ask ourselves: How is a change for the better to be made?" etc. etc.

Here the question which includes everything that is at stake – what the church, the state, the civil government, and the relationship of these three, should be to meet the demands of God's Word – is dismissed, and another is brought to the fore: How can we best bring *our* people back to God and His Word?

This clears the way for the argument that designates Rome to be the natural ally of the Calvinist – my mistake, "the Calvinist" has temporarily disappeared from view – of every positive believer who stands above ecclesiastical division.

This argument runs as follows: Say not: a Protestant state, but a Protestant nation; the great contradiction at the beginning of our century was not Protestant or Roman, but Christian or unchristian; Rome is on our side in the fight against anti-Christianity.

We can stop here. We have arrived at the place we need to be. It was not a question of refuting the articles in *The Standard*, but of indicating the importance of the investigation instituted by the men of "the free church in the free state." And we are admonished by *The Standard* to consider seriously what *The Herald* will teach us about government, the nation, the statutes, the law, etc., in accordance with God's Word!

We can put to one side the remainder of what *The Standard* has to offer us. There is literally nothing in this and the whole of the following argument, regardless of how many beautiful and correct passages it contains, that the writer, when taking his assurances one by one into account, would not be obliged to take back. True Protestantism celebrates Christ as the Head of the church, and the King of the kings of the earth. But for this reason it does not tolerate a vicar of Christ on earth, it ascribes to the church only a ministering power, and makes the civil government dependent solely on God. True Protestantism bows to the authority of God's Word. That is precisely why it does not make common cause with Rome but opposes it, in the 19th as well as in the 16th century, because Rome denies in all manner of ways the Word to which the Reformers have appealed against it. True Protestantism attaches no value to a belief that has not been wrought by the Lord's Spirit, which does not work entirely of its own accord. But that is why it detests both the goal with which Rome seeks to awaken faith, and the means by which it seeks to achieve that goal.

And although it could overlook the gulf which lies between a Protestant nation and Rome, experience has taught us that the latter is not the natural ally of the Protestant, but of the unbeliever. Who helped dechristianize our schools? Who is in league with liberalism in everything that concerns art? Who benefits from the influence and the strength of numbers that they gain, including by our efforts? There is no end to questions.

However, these questions lie in a field that we now leave, to surrender ourselves to the guidance of *The Herald*. It would be very surprising to us if what it should derive from Scripture would not gain our consent. Conversely, it should not be difficult to indicate the nature, the extent, and the grounds of the difference.

1. SURVEY OF THE TERRAIN

The Herald of February 4th, 1900,[35] contains the first of a new series of articles which have yet to be completed, which, under the heading "church and state" are to form a coherent and, as far as possible, complete argument.

The viewpoints of Dr. Kuyper regarding the mutual relationship between the two institutions are well-known. Recently in the Stone Lectures, he spoke of having always striven for "A free Church in a free State."[36]

We believe we know what this means. It is the slogan of Cavour,[37] which in our view only has its place in a Roman Catholic country, not a Protestant one. For the moment we will leave that to one side; although how this viewpoint can be tailored to the system of divinity advocated by Dr. Kuyper, is a mystery to us. We do not understand how these considerations of statecraft are really compatible with the Scriptural data, and with the Calvinistic dogmatic, ecclesiastical, and church-legal principle.

The articles in question promise a fundamental presentation of all the issues relating to this. Reason enough to welcome with particular interest this final series on "Common Grace" in *The Herald*. We might, with a word of thanks, proceed to the investigation and discussion, if it were not for the fact that some of the things mentioned in the introductory article attracted our attention, as they directly indicate that the writer is working with principles and concepts which, from the perspective of a purely Reformed position, cannot be accepted at face value.

---

[35] [See the appendix for issue numbers, with corresponding chapter numbers as they are found in *Common Grace,* vol. 3.]

[36] Abraham Kuyper, *Lectures on Calvinism* (Grand Rapids, MI: Wm. B. Eerdmans Publishing Co., 1931 [1898]), p. 99.

[37] [Camillo Benso, Count of Cavour (1810–1861), Italian statesman who led the movement toward the unification of Italy.]

Inappropriate Parameters of Inquiry

The first thing that strikes us is that the writer intends to speak on "church and state." Then, as the discussion progresses, he replaces the concept "state" with the concept "civil government" [Overheid] so as to bring it into line with Article 36. But the concept "church" expands the horizon to Articles 27–35. He is perhaps free to do this. But he is not free to bind others to this arrangement. Especially since the actual objection to the writer's viewpoint concerns Article 36.

After all, if and insofar as the issue does extend that far [i.e., to the doctrine of the church], it is anything but desirable to put such a demand on his interlocutors at the start, since the purpose now is not so much to ascertain a difference but to find agreement, to the degree that such is possible. Even less so because what is involved is the same blurring of boundaries which has had such baneful consequences both on the terrain of church and school and in the area of the state, and with the same confusion that one might have hoped finally could be avoided, when a few men of rank indicted themselves at the [Nonconformist] Synod of Middelburg and invoked a church judgement upon themselves.[38]

The requirement, immediately stated in the introduction to the series on "church and state," that those who object to a purported deviation in the Confession from now on are to appeal exclusively to a systematic exposition of notions *on which this deviation is based,* must be challenged from the outset, to keep the latter error from becoming worse than the first.

This is not looking for a pretext to start an argument. It is laying the axe at the root of the error. Now that the aberrant opinion regarding Article 36 has finally been submitted to the judgment of the church [at the Middelburg synod],

---

[38] [See pp. 20f. above. As will become clear in the subsequent discussion, Kuyper, by choosing to defend his position regarding Article 36 in a series of articles on "church and state," blurs the issue, because Article 36 – as he himself indicates in no. 1154 – speaks of religion, not the church strictly speaking.]

one needs to take his stand [in that forum] and vindicate his right to deviate in such a manner. If those who left the national church in 1886 had not [prejudged the issue in their favor and] extended to themselves certificates of fidelity and orthodoxy, they would have sought a different, more regular solution to the ecclesiastical question. For one cannot deny a right to others that one demands for oneself.[39]

This is true in particular with regard to the right to deviate from the Confession. On the Reformed standpoint, this right presupposes both the normative authority of God's Word and the dogmatic authority of ecclesiastical assemblies. Does this not condemn the Separation of 1834, at least in its radical version; does it not condemn the Nonconformity?

We may firmly state that a person or association lacks the right to establish the principles that may be derived from the Confession, as long as the church has not expressed itself on the preliminary question.

This relates to the issue that came up at the meeting at the Seinpost Hotel.[40] That a system built upon those illegitimate principles, even upon that Confession-deviating opinion, finds application, e.g., in a political party,[41] is but an appetizer, and in my view lies in the nature of the case. But of course, we do not

---

[39] [i.e., the Nonconformists demanded conformity to the Three Forms of Unity from the modernists, and when this could not be worked out, they separated from the church; but when it came to their own deviation from the Three Forms, they avoided the issue.]

[40] [A reference to Kuyper's stage-managed denunciation of De Savornin Lohman at the annual meeting of the Association for Higher Education, held at the Seinpost Hotel in Scheveningen in 1895, precipitating the latter's dismissal from the Free University for supposed deviation from the "Reformed Basis" of the school. This "Reformed Basis" by this time had been unilaterally determined and settled by Kuyper himself, with the help of his allies, including Herman Bavinck, in violation of the Association's bylaws. See further Dr. J. Stellingwerff, *Dr. Abraham Kuyper en de Vrije Universiteit* [Dr. Abraham Kuyper and the Free University] (Kampen: J. H. Kok, 1987), pp. 200ff.]

[41] [A reference to the Anti-Revolutionary Party.]

have to deal with such irregularities in this connection. We said all we needed to say about it in "A Preliminary Word" above. Yet Dr. Kuyper's demand that those who challenge his deviation from the Confession, in particular "the well-known clause in Article 36," from now on must exclusively appeal to a treatment that lies in entirely different terrain, proceeds from the same presupposition that is responsible for the Nonconformity.[42] This is the reason for the above-mentioned reminder, and the subjoined protest.

A question of philosophical discussion or scriptural investigation?

What exactly did Dr. Kuyper do in this introduction to his series of articles on "church and state"?

With the utmost sincerity, he denied that Article 36 "in its most well-known clause" is affirmed by him. In our view this should have the consequence that he announce his intention once and for all to make clear that, deviating from the Confession, he has returned to Holy Scripture. But no. We instead hear the complaint that those who accuse him of being a kindred spirit of the men of the French Revolution, who maintain that he trafficked with the Liberals, simply overlooked "what he positively put forth in contradiction thereto;" the announcement, that over a period of twenty years or more had used a few less felicitous expressions for which he was still being persecuted; and the demand that his opponents limit themselves to consulting *this* treatment as the authentic and documented evidence of his views, now that he finally has had occasion to express himself on the matter at hand.

Had Dr. Kuyper not said in the same context that "a fundamental exposition of the question with a view to history, a view to circumstances of the time, and a view to the future, should not be left undone," and so indicated that he would indeed discuss in his argumentation what is related to the theological side of the question, which is what we are interested in, then we would have considered the periphrastic account provided in the introduction to be

---

[42] [The gist of the complaint is, Kuyper arrogates to himself the right to establish his own terms for judging, instead of submitting to proper procedure in the proper forum.]

electioneering ahead of the upcoming campaign,[43] which should be left to his own account.

For if the entire disagreement between us and Dr. Kuyper comes down to what he here says and suggests, then we would gladly leave the further treatment of this matter to those who revel in quibbles, who aim to catch others in the web of their own words, who pass over what lies close at hand in order to go back twenty years or more to take advantage of a poorly chosen usage. But that is *not* what is going on here.

Dr. Kuyper's political viewpoints are well-known. They can be derived just as well from *Sphere Sovereignty*[44] as from *Our Program*,[45] as well from *Iron and Clay*[46] as from *Not the Freedom Tree but the Cross*,[47] as well from the *Lectures on Calvinism* as from.... whatever he has written, whether a long time ago or not.

His viewpoint touches on the Confession mainly with regard to the vocation and competence of the civil magistrate, together with the sources of the knowledge by which the civil magistrate is to function. It is said that a zoologist can surmise the build of a completely unknown prehistoric animal from a fragment of its skeleton. Now then: One single statement concerning the work and the office of the civil magistrate, expressed in whatever form, provides anyone who thinks things through, with the opportunity to investigate what follows by logical consequence for the related parts of his system.

This objection is based on one yet more fundamental to the scope of the argument provided in *The Herald*. The author complains, as we heard, that his critics pay too much attention to his dispute with Article 36 and take too little notice of his positive statements against liberalism. He had no right to adduce

---

[43] [A reference to the political campaign for the Second Chamber, which resulted in Kuyper becoming Prime Minister. See n. 33.]

[44] [*Souvereiniteit in eigen kring* (Amsterdam: J. H. Kruyt, 1880).]

[45] [*Ons Program* (Amsterdam: J. H. Kruyt, 1879). English translation: *Our Program*, trans. Harry van Dyke (Bellingham, WA: Lexham Press, 2015). The translations here provided are made directly from the original, not taken from the Lexham Press edition.]

[46] [*IJzer en leem* (Amsterdam: J. H. Kruyt, 1885).]

[47] [*Niet de vrijheidsboom maar het kruis* (Amsterdam: J. A. Wormser, 1889).]

any such positive statements, but above all, as already stated, to provide the evidence that Article 36 does not agree with Holy Scripture.

We position ourselves on the Reformed ecclesiastical standpoint. For the confusion of which we spoke above does not consist in the provision by Dr. Kuyper of a treatment of the true mutual relation between church and state, but in his wish to demonstrate *by that treatment* that he has the right to deviate from the church's Confession, and *by that treatment* seeks to convince those who do not.

Allow us to elaborate. Article 36 of the Belgic Confession does not treat "of Common Grace." Nor "of Church and State." But "of the Office of the Civil Magistrate." This indicates the terrain in which we have to function in this issue. This terrain is even more restricted by the nature of the suspicions brought against this article by the Reformed Nonconformists. Because everything that here concerns the good right of the civil magistrate, or of the origin thereof, remains outside the field of view. It is not disputed. What most certainly is to be investigated is whether the magistrate has a task with regard to "the preaching of the gospel," "the expansion of the Kingdom of God," "the struggle against error," "the maintenance of the worship service," etc.

Regardless of the question as to how one is to understand the statements of Article 36 in terms of the rules of grammatical, historical, or dogmatic exegesis, there is the fact that our church charges the magistrate with things for which, according to both Revolutionaries and Anti-Revolutionaries, it is not authorized. This is what the issue is all about. This difference may not be trivialized. Judgment of the past, policy for the present, and the relation of church and state in the future depend on this.

It is simply the question: are they right who deem that our fathers had not yet freed themselves from Roman Catholic influences when they conferred on the magistrate the power to judge in matters of religion? We expected to hear Dr. Kuyper treat of this with the goal of educating us, if after our investigation he should prove to have been right. This explains our disappointment.

The fatal flaw in the entire framework of Dr. Kuyper's discussion lies in this, that 1) forgetting his position and the Reformed church-legal standpoint, he builds on terrain that is inappropriate; and furthermore that 2) he works with two concepts that at the very least give rise to misunderstanding, and run the risk of answering the question in favor of more modern viewpoints, simply by the way in which it is posed.

If Dr. Kuyper wishes to speak of "church and state," perhaps we also, incidentally, will get to hear something about the actual question, how his viewpoint rhymes with the Confession and finally with Scripture. But if he says: I will provide a "fundamental exposition" of this clause in the Confession, and desire that you refer only to this exposition in your evaluation, we are obliged to answer: We would like to take your building into consideration, but if you tell us that had we paid more attention to the building, we would not have had to pay so much attention to the foundations – well, then this would be a good time to check and see whether there are any cracks in the walls.

The conclusion to these considerations is this: we are obliged to leave out of our purview as irrelevant everything in Dr. Kuyper's discussion that does not serve to justify his standpoint regarding Article 36. Since, however, it is unfair and, in the end, impossible to assess the individual parts of a system outside the framework in which they are fitted, we are obliged to take the discussion as it is put forward here, pointing out what in our opinion is subject to misgiving; and when all the data have been collected in this manner, we will conduct further investigation on the specific points where necessary. We would otherwise easily be distracted from the main issues, and, even if we did not ourselves lose sight of the purpose, we would run the danger of fatiguing others. For with an argumentation, as with a depiction on canvas, the effect depends very much on what artists call "perspective."

Regarding the explanation of Article 36,[48] we are entirely in agreement with the author, that

> the words ... 'And their office is, not only to have regard unto and watch for the welfare of the civil state, but also that they protect the sacred ministry, and thus may remove and prevent all idolatry and false worship; that the kingdom of antichrist may be thus destroyed, and the kingdom of Christ promoted. They must,

---

[48] In issue no. 1154 of *The Herald*.

therefore, countenance the preaching of the word of the gospel every where, that God may be honored and worshiped by every one, as he commands in his Word'[49] cannot and should not be understood as the liberation of the church and the extension to it of moral support, but doubtless refer to an obligation to defend the true church, if necessary, with the sword.

We here nevertheless already run into a characterization which lines up with the spirit of Kuyper's thought, but which, however benign it appears, would directly introduce a confusing element into the discussion.

Which Church does Article 36 have in mind?

One can speak of the "church" in more than one sense; normally one distinguishes between the visible, the invisible, and the instituted church. The Confession, however, speaks of the *true* and the *false* church. This categorization assumes that the church is one and undivided, and consequently already contradicts what presents itself to us in reality, a church which has denied its principle, the church in its pluriformity. This leads to a confusion of concepts. Which is why we need to remind ourselves 1) that Article 36 does not speak of the church, but of the kingdom of the Antichrist and the kingdom of Christ, and 2) that according to this article it is not opinions that deviate from the Confession, not errors, even gross errors, but only "idolatry and false worship" which are to be removed, and 3) that in the article there is no mention at all of "defending the church."

---

[49] [The quoted text of Article 36 is taken from Philip Schaff, *The Creeds of Christendom,* vol. 3 (New York: Harper & Brothers, 1882), p. 432. Attached to it is the following footnote, written by Schaff: "This section, like the corresponding sections in other Reformed Confessions, is framed on the theory of a union of Church and State, and is applicable to Free Churches only so far as they may justly claim from the civil government legal protection in all their rights." Evidently, Kuyper's errors were not restricted to him. As Hoedemaker notes on p. 37, "The state-church cannot be defended with an appeal to the Confession."]

It is self-evident that the civil magistrate must defend the rights of its subjects and that above all it must not hinder them in the performance of their duties. This principle also benefits the church. From this it can even be deduced that the church is not to be put on a level with other associations, and that it must be of public right. But this idea is not in the Confession, and did not need to be expressed explicitly. The state-church cannot be defended with an appeal to the Confession, and Dr. Kuyper apparently has the state-church in mind.

But one can go even further. The civil magistrate is to uphold the holy worship service and ensure that the Word of the gospel is preached, but with the specific and express goal "that God may be honored and worshiped by every one, as he commands in his Word." This draws the line between the purpose of the church, "the edifying of the body of Christ" [Ephesians 4: 12] in administering the church service, and the vocation of the magistrate.

What does it Mean to "Bear the Sword" in Matters of Religion?

Be that as it may, let us turn to the objection raised by Dr. Kuyper in his discussion. He is entirely justified when he writes: "The civil magistrate is a power ordained of God, clothed with derived sovereignty over all citizens, a power that 'beareth the sword' and consequently implements its will with coercion and the strong arm if need be. If it is said of such a power that it must remove and prevent something, then that cannot be understood other than as removal and prevention with the strong arm if need be."

Crystal clear. If we had not known that the writer is an advocate of Reformed principles, we would be inclined to infer that such clarity is the consequence of his independent position vis-à-vis the Confession. The more repellently the challenged article in the Confession is presented, the less difficulty there is in justifying its rejection!

Such a consideration could have hindered the author from moving so bitingly against those who have attempted to make Article 36 amenable for modern conceptions, not by rejecting it but by interpreting it. He pillories in a way that betrays no intention to spare the opponent, an anonymous author who had the courage to suggest that the magistrate might perhaps fulfill the task entrusted to him according to Article 36 by offering only moral support to the church.

This explanation, says Kuyper, if applied consistently, would lead to the complete denial of our Christian faith. For it does not ask how the fathers intended this or that, but how can we explain it so that it conforms to our opinions? This explanation is in conflict with all concepts of honesty and good faith.

In our view, the anonymous author might respond, "Dost not thou fear God, seeing thou art in the same condemnation?" [Luke 23: 40]. It is possible to take the view that the magistrate must promote religion by moral means, so that by such use it fulfills its obligation in a much better way than if it were to use coercive power in the old-fashioned way, and yet not violate the laws of honesty and good faith.

If we were not restricted to the articles in *The Herald*, we could appeal to Dr. Kuyper to bear witness in favor of the anonymous author. On page 50 of *Honor is Delicate*,[50] he writes to W. H. de Beaufort:

> And do you ask me whether I would like the magistrate, who after all holds a conviction in my system, to consider with indifference the development of religion, of morality and of science? If I did, then my old friend Dr. Hoedemaker would be perfectly right, that my place was on your side in the field of Revolution; in this case, not with regard to the illiberal practice of your kindred spirits, but with regard to the principle.
>
> But this is certainly not my point of view. On the contrary, in my view the magistrate is by all means called to ensure that the true religion flourishes, that the morality ordained by God prospers, and that true science grows in ripeness. If it turned out, then, that the magistrate, through his active action, promoted true religion, irrigated decent morality, and cultivated true science, I would without hesitation regard it as his duty to take that path.

Is this not virtually the same thing as what he just got done pillorying?

But in the same essay in which blows are dealt out to the anonymous author, he makes an excellent plea for Prof. van Velzen, "who softened the meaning of

---

[50] *Eer is Teer: Tegen Mr. W. H. de Beaufort's Gidsartikel "de deputatenvergadering"* [Honor is Delicate: Against W. H. de Beaufort's article in *De Gids* regarding the assembly of deputies] (Amsterdam: J. A. Wormser, 1889).

the familiar phrase from Article 36 out of pious reverence" and even found a proof in this that Van Velzen wished to stick to the Confession. "It must be said in honor of the aforementioned" – and in this there indeed lies a difference between him, i.e., Van Velzen, and the anonymous author – "that he in principle advocated the restoration of government interference."

Removal and prevention take place with violence if need be – we are in full agreement with the author on this. But this remark overthrows Dr. Kuyper's further discussion. For when the author claims that "Article 36, in particular the most familiar clause of that article, introduces a foreign element into the Belgic Confession," this entails that that which in accordance with this article is entrusted to the magistrate, is in flagrant contradiction with the other parts of the Confession. Is this the case? What, according to the Belgic Confession, must the magistrate remove and prevent?

Violence in matters of faith?

At the end of this initial article in which Dr. Kuyper passes in review his main viewpoints regarding Article 36, he joins those who "consider violence on the part of the magistrate in matters of faith to be in conflict with Scripture." He thus says here that the Reformed church in its Confession officially taught that "violence in matters of faith" is permitted and in agreement with Scripture.

We will have to scrutinize this statement at the appropriate time and place. According to Dr. Kuyper, it is based on the following rationale: "This sentiment such as was quoted above was nearly universal in the days in which the Confession was drawn up. It was the sentiment of the Lutheran, of the Roman Catholic, and of the Reformed." The latter is proved by an appeal to Calvin's tract regarding Servetus' death sentence, and to "that which is to be read about this point of dispute in the older dogmatic writings of the Reformed side."

He continues:

This entire system was not a new discovery by the Reformed but the general sentiment of their time, against which *only a few voices were raised in protest. It was the theory of Rome* which was maintained for centuries, the error of which one did not yet discern. *One drifted along with the current of the past* and defended the received sentiment *with the same arguments with which it has always been professed.*

One therefore cannot say that our fathers parroted the Roman opinion half-consciously. That was not the case. It was a received opinion which they themselves approved of, advocated, and broadly defended.

We have taken the liberty of italicizing a few expressions which merit attention. Now for a few explanatory notes.

Calvin is said to have advocated violence in matters of faith. There is nothing, or nearly nothing, to this. We will consult the aforementioned treatise about it. Should the author – may it never be! – prove to have understood Calvin properly on this point, then perhaps we will be given a statement regarding that which continues to be a mystery to us, namely, his sympathy, even in politics, for Calvinism.

The same holds true for the older divines. Dr. Kuyper neglected to mention which "voices" against violence in matters of faith were raised. We have to fill this void and provide the evidence that the opinion of the dissenters most certainly was connected to their dogmatics, and that those dogmatics and the principles flowing therefrom were opposed by the fathers on Scriptural grounds.

One question remains, whether it was "the theory of Rome" that our fathers adopted? If they had not opposed that theory, the opinion of Dr. Kuyper on this point would not be condemned out of hand. What is going on here? This man of science has neglected to follow the footsteps of our divines in their distinction between the freedom to believe and the freedom to profess, between the freedom to practice religion and the freedom to propagandize, to blaspheme, to undermine the foundations of society and state, to swear allegiance to a foreign prince, to exercise rule, etc.

Only when this omission is repaired is it possible to find an explanation for two facts of which the author is here honest enough to make mention:

1) "Those who in those days were in danger of becoming victims to this system, nevertheless never in the least thought to cast doubt on this confession."

A remarkable phenomenon. With the heretics, it was precisely the opposite. With the Anabaptists as well, in their day.

2) "The conflict with their deeper-lying principles only gradually came to light in practice, and to awareness in Reformed life. For notwithstanding that our fathers agreed unanimously with Article 36, including that difficult clause,

the Netherlands became the cradle, not of persecution because of faith, but of freedom of conscience."

Thus, according to Dr. Kuyper, Article 36 teaches coercion of conscience.

It is absolutely necessary to subject these assertions to a closer investigation. If we knew nothing more of Dr. Kuyper's opinion, we would say to ourselves upon reading this essay: his rejection of Article 36 of the Belgic Confession is simply the consequence of a misunderstanding that can speedily be resolved. Perhaps the evidence from our history would then serve to that end, the evidence that our fathers did not, as he suspects, go "from the scaffold to the placards, and from the placards to a practice that conflicts with those placards," except that here there is no question of evolution and not even of changed practice, unless the "fathers" of whom he speaks are the libertine and Remonstrant regents, whose indifference, connivance with Popery, and allowance of pagan abominations were always challenged by our divines.

What if that difficult clause in Article 36 showed that *it is precisely persecution on account of faith that is ruled out?* We hope to provide the evidence that the opinion unjustly attributed to our fathers was in conflict not only with the underlying principles of the Reformed church, but with the entire Confession in its most obvious teachings. The civil government had to fulfill everything commissioned to it on its own terrain, public life. It was no lord of conscience, no taskmaster of faith. The public interpretation of Scripture was not entrusted to it. But neither was it the mere executor of the church's commands; it made use of the church's advice in accordance with its own judgement.

Dr. Kuyper is mistaken when he attributes this opinion to the fathers, and therefore also when he attributes attachment to this opinion to the desire for imitation.

In short: Above we laid out the line by which, to the degree it proves necessary, this conclusion soon will be confirmed in all aspects. Only to the degree it proves necessary, because we harbor no illusions, as if removing the objection brought forward by Dr. Kuyper would clear the way to a joint brotherly opinion between those who demand that the civil government not interfere with the church and religion, and those who consider neutrality in the affairs of religion, even and not least in the sphere in which the magistrate rules as God's viceroy, to be an absurdity.

For even if it were obvious that the fathers of the Reformed church did not consider "violence by the magistrate in matters of faith" to be appropriate, even if our argumentation on this point were impeccable, and our conclusion in this case proved to be so cogent that every opponent would have to yield, it would not give us anything useful to the purpose at hand. Why not? Because the actual objection to the political view that agrees with Article 36, and the actual reasons for that contrary opinion, have nothing to do with this question. In fact, they lie outside the Confession and are of such a character that they fall not only outside Scripture, but render impotent the witness directly from the Old Testament and indirectly from the New Testament.

The Root of the Error: The Wrong Concept of the Church

Is this saying too much? No, it is saying too little. We here are confronted with a system that owes its rise to an error of logic, to wit, to the establishment of the *conclusion* in the form of an apparently benign *definition*, that of the church.

In issue no. 1155 of *The Herald*, one finds a description of the concept "church." The characteristics of this church, however, are taken not from Scripture but from abnormal reality. Dr. Kuyper means the church, not as it should be according to God's Word, but as it now manifests itself. To wit:

> A phenomenon manifests itself in the terrain of the state which goes by the name of Church, and is called Church by the people in the vernacular.
>
> Whether one wishes to call such a church a society, a club, a partnership, or whatever, is a matter of indifference to us in this context. It is not that we should consider the true and particular significance of the concept of the church to be a matter of indifference, but in this discussion, it has no influence on the relation as far as the state goes.

Thus saith Dr. Kuyper. He consequently has in mind the church not in its actual essence but in its temporal form of appearance. "The church not as organism, but as institute."

"By the church as institute, we understand a circle of persons living in the same relation, which express this relation in a written confession and a specific church order." It is self-evident that he does not find this church in the Old Testament: not in the period of the patriarchs, because [according to him] no profession was made, and there was no membership and no ecclesiastical office; not in the Mosaic and post-Mosaic period, because while ecclesiastical office and public worship did exist, one belonged to this church not because of profession, but because of the affiliation of the Israelite to the people of Israel under Israelite statehood.

Now the student of the Heidelberg Catechism obviously forms a completely different idea of the church. It is the congregation that Christ gathers by His Word and Spirit unto eternal life, a congregation that has existed from the beginning of the world (21st Sunday).

Dr. Kuyper obscures the contradiction between the two conceptions with the remark that the "Catechist could not here have intended the church as institute, since one does not remain a member of this eternally. The Lutheran, the Reformed, and all the other churches removes the dead from the list of its members." That is self-evident. But what does it prove? That his conception is wrong. A church existed which was not instituted in the sense given by Dr. Kuyper. A civil government existed together with this non-instituted church. We thus need to investigate the mutual rights and duties that this church and this state had with each other.

Note well! We do not wish to place ourselves outside reality. One should also speak of the relation of the magistrate 1) to the institute, 2) to the church in its abnormal condition, the church in its pluriformity. But these questions are secondary. The primary question is, what does Scripture have to say about this matter 1) in the Old Testament, 2) in the New Testament? We are now occupied with the Old Testament, and above all will provide the evidence that from the start, *The Herald* has erred in a cardinal point. For it appeals to the composition of the Sanhedrin and the constitution of the synagogue, and to the confusion of the ecclesiastical and civil power in both. It is thus a simple matter to refute him on these points.

The appeal to the Sanhedrin and the synagogue is irrelevant because they pertain to the extra-scriptural development of the Jewish people. By contrast, during the patriarchal, Mosaic, and post-Mosaic period, the distinction between the subjects – citizens and members – the offices, officers, sphere of operation etc. can be clearly delineated.[51]

In *The Herald* we come up against the same confusion between the essence of the church and its form of appearance that led to the Nonconformity. It is as if someone commencing an investigation into the history of clothing would say, "By clothing, I mean a gentleman in a sport coat or suit, or a lady in a ballroom dress or a gown," in order to avoid any connection to the animal skins in the Garden of Eden.

The apparently benign definition provided in *The Herald* at the start of the discussion of "the relation between church and state," is central to the range of deviations which may be toned down by Dr. Kuyper but which are anything but benign. The identification of church and state in the Old Covenant is purely Anabaptist, while the identification of the form of appearance and the essence of the church in the institute is purely Roman Catholic.

That Dr. Kuyper cannot be absolved of this – speaking of the last-mentioned case – appears from the complete break in his viewpoint between the Old and the New Testament. The church, he says, "first arose as an independent ecclesiastical institution through the call by Jesus of the twelve apostles, His investing them with official power, etc." When the apostolate in this manner is turned into an office in the church, we have episcopacy with the primacy of Peter, i.e., the papacy, in the bud. We hope to provide evidence that the institution of the apostolate stands in connection with the *kingship* of the Savior, and not with His activity as Head of the congregation.[52]

A logical error is concealed in the definition, "we take the church as organism, not institute," which in fact presumes the result at which the author wishes to arrive. The church as institute is the church with all its organizational paraphernalia, the church not only embodied, but also clothed. If we demonstrate that the civil magistrate may not interfere with the organization of that church, and with its constitution and relation to other churches, have we at the same

---

[51] We have already done this in *Sword and Trowel* [Troffel en Zwaard] (Utrecht: J. Bijleveld, 1898), vol. 1.

[52] [For a thorough exposition of this line of reasoning, see Hoedemaker, *Reformed Ecclesiology*.]

time demonstrated that the magistrate has nothing to do with its confession, more specifically with that part of it that influences the outside world? While the magistrate may not prescribe what the church must believe, teach, or preach, may the magistrate not hinder the church from proclaiming that it alone has the right to appoint and dismiss government officials, to undermine the foundations of law and morality, and the like?

In this we neither affirm nor deny anything, but only note that the question in *The Herald,* including that which concerns the New Testament, is not properly stated when, in agreement with the provided definition, it is posed in the following manner: "When Jesus invested the twelve apostles with official power, the world church (?) arose in its local independent institutes (?) and the question arose as to how the relation of these institutes to the state institution was to be arranged." It would seem that Dr. Kuyper cannot stop thinking about the question of the separation of church and state. But in our view, it was for an entirely different reason that the church came into conflict with the Jewish and the pagan magistrate, and the magistrate knew nothing of a "church institute." Yet we continually run the risk of forgetting that our task in this chapter is only to determine the points of difference which will shortly be investigated in order to inform our final conclusion. There is so much to learn from Dr. Kuyper's argument and style of reasoning!

For example, the question is also raised here as to whether the truth is of two sorts, one for politics, another for theology. Or whether, on the basis of the Reformed standpoint (what are we saying? The standpoint of those for whom God's Word is the rule of faith and life) one may claim at one moment that "your church is not a church but an association!" and at another, "it makes no difference if one considers the church to be a club, or views it as an association!" Another thing at stake here is whether the Confession may be laid at the foundation of higher education, and thus the scientific pursuit of state law.

Let us go on. Having traversed a terrain full of pitfalls, we now breathe a sigh of relief because we follow our guide into an entirely different terrain, that of the state. We can adopt entirely the framework in which he places church and state in order to indicate the difference between the two. The "point of origin for the life of the state lies in the things originally created." The state lies in the terrain of natural life for us as well. If God withholds the light of His special revelation from the magistrate, he remains the magistrate, God's viceroy, even though he walks by the light of nature.

But when Dr. Kuyper claims the Word for the church, and says that its point of origin, naturally in distinction to that of the civil government, lies in the Word, then this presupposes a conception of common and particular grace, as well as of church and state, that we find unacceptable.

Defining Common and Particular Grace

Special revelation, in our view, includes not only everything that concerns atonement, i.e., the restoration of communion between God and man, but everything that touches on atonement in the broader sense, to wit, the restoration, indeed the glorification of the initial creation. And particular grace does not coincide so completely with the Word and with atonement that one may assign common grace to the terrain of the state, and particular grace to that of the church. In our view, this is to say too much and too little at the same time: the former is at bottom Anabaptist and, consistently carried through, Roman Catholic; the latter robs the church of a portion of its sphere, the vocation to administer the Word to peoples and governments.

With regard to the former: Our fathers did not understand the expression "particular grace" in exactly the same way that we find over and over again in Dr. Kuyper's discussion. For example, Wilhelmus à Brakel in his *The Christian's Reasonable Service* speaks of grace in this manner:

> Grace is either common or particular. God bestows common grace upon all men by granting them temporal benefits.... To this grace also belongs all the good which God bestows upon all who are called, by giving them the Word—the means unto repentance and salvation.... In addition to this, God generally gives illumination, historical faith, convictions, and inner persuasion to almost become a Christian (cf. Heb 6:4–6).
>
> Particular grace is the effectual call whereby man is illuminated with wondrous spiritual light, effectually changing his will, and thus in very deed

translating him out of darkness into light, out of death to life, and from the dominion of sin and the devil to Christ and His kingdom.[53]

As far as the latter is concerned: God has called the church to enlighten the magistracies. For this purpose, the public interpretation of the Word is entrusted to it. Should one silence the church in this without ascribing to the state the competence to ascertain the truth, then one of necessity will have to relegate the state as much as possible to the terrain, not only of natural life stemming from the original creation, but quite specifically to the extra-religious, to the observable.

We discern this tendency very clearly in the description of "the sphere," "the power" (*The Herald* speaks of "the resources"), "the character," "the vocation" and "the final goal of the magistracy." The state, according to *The Herald,* deals with land and water, bridges and roads, money and possessions, protection of property and decency, while the church considers man as sinner and redeemed.

The deviation starts with the establishment of the starting point. As if the magistrate is not established, called, and instructed by the Word! God clothed man with judicial authority, which until then He exercised directly, when He spoke the word, "Whoso sheddeth man's blood, by man shall his blood be shed" (Genesis 9: 6). There is also a Noahic Covenant.

Dr. Kuyper too knows this quite well. In various contexts, he states that the civil government originates in special revelation and is not so bound to the natural knowledge of God that it cannot make use of that special revelation which comes to it through the intermediation of public opinion. But this does not hinder him from nullifying Scripture regarding the origin of the magistracy, by remarking that the command of the Noahic covenant coincides with the voice of nature in blood vengeance, and that the promise of this covenant only preserves from destruction that which exists. Neither the one nor the other is to the point. The greater includes the lesser.[54] Furthermore, this only touches on

---

[53] *The Christian's Reasonable Service,* trans. Bartel Elshout, ed. Joel R. Beeke, vol. 2 (Grand Rapids, MI: Reformation Heritage Books, 1993), p. 215.

[54] [In other words, this "voice of nature" (the lesser) is also direct revelation from God (the greater).]

the form in which God's command comes to His creatures. All of this lies in the area of definitions.

The second part of the essay, commencing in no. 1159, nevertheless shows us the value of these definitions for the question regarding the proper relation between church and state. We are again told that the magistrate can walk by the light of nature, and also that a pagan magistrate is owed obedience just as much as a Christian ruler is. But then comes the question, what is it that changes for the state, should the light of "particular grace" begin to shine in a country "over which a non-Christian magistracy rules?"

Outstanding things are given in answer to this question, in an exceptionally outstanding manner. "The gospel tells us not only what we must do to be saved. Godliness is useful in all things.... The Bible expresses itself about the basic concepts of state, penal, and commercial law. It straightens out warped principles." In fact, however good much of what Dr. Kuyper has said in this vein may be, it is impossible to lay out the magistrate's obligation to rule according to the Word of God in a more just, beautiful, and sharply delineated manner than he does in issue no. 1160.

Those who say that he considers the light of the natural knowledge of God to be sufficient for the civil government, and consequently does not bind it to God's revealed will, do so mistakenly. To wit:

> Certainly, every notion as if the revelation of God asserts its claim only in a limited terrain must be decisively combatted; and never was the author done greater wrong than when he was attributed the opinion that the revelation of the Word was only valid for believers, so that in the political field there could only be reckoned with the natural knowledge of God. We know how that notion entered into the world, but we do not yet understand how skilled writers came to impute such an opinion to us as if it expressed our serious opinion. Anything more than a superficial acquaintance with what we have published in all kinds of ways should have spared us from such an allegation....

Let no one further attribute to Dr. Kuyper the ridiculous idea that he wishes to render the magistrate, God's servant, independent of the Lord's revealed will! Duly noted.

The Magistrate Restricted to the Natural Knowledge of God

It suffices us now to report that we would be in entire agreement with Dr. Kuyper in this, if he did not prove too much. "Anything more than a superficial acquaintance with what we have published in all kinds of ways should have spared us from such an allegation," says Dr. Kuyper. Hereby he speaks not only of how he *now* thinks with regard to the duty of the magistrate to act according to God's will, but also of how he has *always* adhered to this conviction. "Those who attributed a different conception to him found a greater reception among those who did not read what we have written."

This shows 1) that the opinion challenged by the author may not be listed among the opinions derived – granted, not without an appearance of justice – from "a few less felicitously chosen expressions used by him over a period of more than twenty years;" 2) that everything in Dr. Kuyper's writings that advocate this opinion or appear to lie in the same line of reasoning do not come from the Anti-Revolutionary leader but were [presumably] inserted by an interpolator unknown to us, whom we can designate, in the manner of the scholars who practice modern Scriptural criticism, "L," meaning Liberal or Libertine.

In *Our Program,* this "L" wrote the following:[55]

[The Anti-Revolutionary Party] bases this claim [of the objective existence of God] not on the revealed, but on the natural knowledge of God (the *theologia naturalis*) which can be discerned from that which of God is seen in the creation, above all in man, and not least in the national or popular organism itself.

Here it consciously treads the path of our Reformed divines, who inexorably maintained this 'natural knowledge of God' precisely for the sake of what fell outside the kingdom of heaven, and additionally, we may add, was recently entirely vindicated in this by Max Müller's lectures on religion.

***

This natural knowledge of God, not the revealed knowledge of God, is of a compulsory character for every person. Certainty with regard to the former does

---

[55] Dutch 1879 ed., §§ 50, 51, pp. 187, 188.

not demand what certainty with regard to the latter demands, to wit, supernatural illumination.

For this cause the non-confessing magistrate is authorized and obligated, in a complete and direct sense, to take the first (natural) knowledge of God as official guideline for its action, not the second (revealed).

The latter would only be the case if an extraordinary power, a supernatural organ existed to discern with firm assurance in every case what the revealed knowledge of God demands (!).

But this organ is lacking. And it of necessity is lacking, because this would either spiritualize the state, or make religion worldly.

The magistrate is rooted directly in natural life, and has as such, i.e., directly, thus no other than, a natural knowledge of God, while the kingdom of God is a supernatural kingdom in which the supernatural knowledge of God shines unhindered.

The magistrate knows from this natural knowledge of God: 1. That there is a God; 2. That this living God determines the fate of all that is created, thus also the state; 3. That this all-governing Providence desires justice, and thus is the avenger of all injustice; and 4. That sin is at work among men, regarding which only a superior intervention can effect redemption.[56]

---

[56] [It is remarkable how closely this tracks Hugo Grotius' enumeration of the attributes of God as discernible by nature: "[True religion] consists in four statements: first, God is one; second, God does not pertain to things that are seen, but is a higher being than all others; third, He concerns Himself with our affairs and judges them with the utmost fairness; fourth, He is creator of all nature outside Himself. The Ten Commandments teach these same statements..." although the Ten Commandments were given only to the Jews and do not form part of natural law (Alvarado, *The Debate that Changed the West* (Aalten: Pantocrator Press), pp. 210, 238). Grotius was an Arminian; by contrast, the Calvinist Johannes Althusius spoke of the Ten Commandments as the expression of natural law for all peoples, to be enforced by the magistrate, they having been "renewed and confirmed by Christ our king" (*ibid.*, p. 152).]

On the basis of this knowledge, gained entirely from natural religion, the state arrives at honoring God in its public dealings; calling on God's holy name in its official documents; sanctifying the oath; devoting a day of rest to Him; holding days of prayer during national disasters; administering justice even unto the sword; and giving the gospel free rein.

L. did not hesitate to label this unfounded opinion "Reformed or Puritan," where[57] he speaks of "the political state of the Reformed or Puritan peoples, which, while confessing the living God, builds the state directly on the natural knowledge of God alone; and consequently, would have the magistrate act actively as God's servant in the sphere of the natural knowledge of God, but only passively in the revealed knowledge of God."[58]

Should one consider this "L" hypothesis to be far-fetched, one is left to surmise that since 1877 Dr. Kuyper has not changed his opinion regarding the relation of the magistrate to God and the revelation of His will, but only changed the form in which he presented this opinion, in order to give his opponents less of a grip on him.

Here are a few things that contradict his claim, which although not relevant to the overall discussion, yet warrant an investigation in the indicated direction.

To this end we need to follow the essay in *The Herald* and derive a few theses for our purpose.

1) The revelation of God is not restricted to the Word. There is also a knowledge of God from nature.

Granted.

2) "The revelation in the Word or in the Scripture, is one of the richest items of God's revelation that we possess." It appears from this that it will be necessary to investigate whether we are using the word "revelation" in the same sense as Dr. Kuyper.

---

[57] [By contrast with, on the one hand, the atheist state, and on the other the "theocratic" state of the Roman Catholics and Lutherans, which according to "L" base themselves partly on special revelation.]

[58] *Our Program,* p. 189.

Should someone call sunlight one of the richest items of light, well, that manner of speaking would raise eyebrows.

It seems to us that we are now on the road to the doctrine of *Our Program* as depicted in the citation above.

3) "Scripture provides a complete answer to the questions concerning the salvation of the soul, but only a bit of a sidelight to the exercise of all manner of crafts and sciences, while nature teaches a great deal about this."

Now things are starting to clear up. Dr. Kuyper is merely expressing the same notions in a different way. "Ruler of believers!" spoke a Dervish, "your entirely family will soon die out." And he received 100 lashes for his message. "Ruler of believers!" spoke another. "You will survive your entire family and soon be in paradise." And he was rewarded with 100 sequins. In other words, a great deal depends upon the manner of presentation.

If one calls nature and reason the most important sources of knowledge of truth, one is a rationalist. But it seems to be quite "Reformed" to move the revelation of God in nature to the foreground in this manner. Yet we think we remember that our Confession speaks not of a natural revelation from which the architect and the statesman can draw, but only of how one learns to know *God* from nature and then from Scripture. *C'est autre chose.*

4) In nos. 1163 and 1165, we are led to a negative conclusion. "Much knowledge, much investigation is required to come to know from revelation how the state is to be established and administered."

"Israel's state establishment is no model for us."

"The gospel is not enough for us."

"It is extremely difficult to obtain firmness and certainty with regard to principles."

"Complete unanimity is lacking. Sufficient authority to determine what is true and what is untrue does not exist."

Thus Dr. Kuyper. We must then pose the question: how do we, how does the magistrate acquire the knowledge of truth, the knowledge also of God's will? If we are not mistaken, we have here reached the fork in the road at which we diverge. Kuyper knows of no middle way between Rome's magisterium and the use of Scripture by Tom, Dick, and Harry, as they see fit; [alternatively,] no middle way between quoting Scripture because it sounds good, and the [preliminary] work of science in Scripture and outside it, which precedes the establishment of the principles of, in this case, state law.

There is a middle way, and we hope to indicate it.

Issue no. 1165 discusses the question of the *neutrality* of the magistrate. Another cardinal point in the issue regarding true statecraft. He says, the magistrate must as a matter of course bow before God's revealed will. We answer, outstanding! He adds, but the magistrate lacks the competence and the capacity to do that. We answer, here is where we part ways! He explains why the magistrate cannot be neutral with respect to religious convictions. All the people say, "Amen!" We do him homage for the outstanding and inimitable way in which he demonstrates this. No magistrate is conceivable without the administration of justice. No administration of justice can exist without criminal law. Criminal law which does not decide between good and evil would be no criminal law. What is good and evil has to be determined in such and such a manner, etc. etc. Without wanting to, the magistrate takes sides regarding a principle of faith.[59] Entirely correct and cogent. But then he announces to us that the magistrate is impotent to rule a people otherwise than in agreement with its own conviction... And the engine again begins misfiring. Not because we deny what is said in this essay about the meaning of the expression "Protestant nation." Nor because we do not agree with the evidence that the Liberal magistrate and even the Roman Catholic populace come under the influence of the Protestant Netherlands unknowingly and unwillingly. This is simply beyond contradiction. But because the actual question is lost from view.

When one concedes, as Dr. Kuyper does, that the magistrate must bow before God's revealed will, the question immediately follows, how is the magistrate to know that will? But rather than provide a concise answer to this question, which is the only thing that is relevant here, we find out first that magistrates are also sinners and as such can derive the answer to the question, what must I do to be saved, from the Bible alone. Following upon this one finds, amongst much that is irrelevant, the evidence that public opinion has so much influence on the magistrate!

---

[59] *The Herald,* no. 1169.

Regardless, we may round off our resumé of Dr. Kuyper's essay at this point. The fact is, *The Herald* issue no. 1171 just as solemnly sets aside the principle which it solemnly stated in no. 1160, that the magistrate is absolutely bound to the will of God as revealed in Holy Scripture.

How it is that an advocate of Reformed principles could favor an opinion in the area of statecraft that deviates from the Confession is a riddle that here finds its explanation, as does the more specific starting point of our investigation.

We may now confirm that the difference concerns the sufficiency and perspicuity of Holy Scripture; the purpose for which and the manner in which the Confession is derived from Scripture, along with the value of the Confession; and the essence of the church and its vocation with regard to the magistrate, the people, and science, more specifically with regard to the *public* interpretation of the Word, as distinguished from the *magisterial* interpretation.

Dr. Kuyper is indeed antirevolutionary to the degree that he seeks the source of all authority in God rather than man, and therefore wholeheartedly subscribes to the statement in Romans 13:1, "the powers that be are ordained of God." But he has this in common with the Revolution, that for whatever reason he rejects the binding authority of God's Word on the magistrate.

We thus have before us a curious viewpoint: the magistrate is God's servant, but the servant is incapable and consequently incompetent to investigate and implement the will of the Lord. In the *Herald* article now under discussion,[60] a plethora of examples are given of people who have certain duties to fulfill but who are kept from doing so by circumstances. A father is to educate his children, but he cannot if he is persecuted, imprisoned, or burned at the stake for the sake of the faith. A passer-by needs to try to save an unhappy one who has fallen in the water, but if he is bound up, he must resign himself to the inevitable and let the victim drown. The conclusion is that the magistrate, if he could, would have to fulfill the will of God as revealed in Scripture, which is to say, if those circumstances or those reasons had not forbidden it.

We will anticipate with great interest the grounds upon which such a remarkable opinion rest. And so we are pleased to note that these are provided with the appropriate level of detail in the most recent articles in the series.

---

[60] *The Herald,* no. 1171.

In anticipation of the upcoming investigation, we may already observe with great satisfaction that the injustice of which Dr. Kuyper complains in no. 1160 of *The Herald* is not so very serious after all.[61] There were those who attributed the notion to him that the magistrate is only considered to be bound to *the natural knowledge of God*. Unjustly, it seemed. This should have been known from the sentences quoted above, as well as the many others that indicate just as clearly that the magistrate may seek the rationale for his conduct nowhere else than from God. This should also have brought the conviction that the assurance which Dr. Kuyper rejects as a serious accusation, indeed testifies of such a lack of insight that one might rather suspect malice aforethought.

But even the most superficial glance at issue no. 1171 shows that Dr. Kuyper has only exchanged an entirely untenable position for one that is just as untenable but also more unassailable. There is no *material* difference between the opinion that is challenged in no. 1160 and the one that is laid out in no. 1171. The claim was that, according to Dr. Kuyper's system, the magistrate operated only on the terrain of *general revelation*. The claim should have been made that, according to this system, the magistrate is also bound to the will of God as revealed in Scripture, but that factually, i.e., in practice, it *could* only act according to the light of nature.

The matter stands something like this: a competitor claims that a certain industrialist works only by hand and not with steam engines, but is set straight by the testimony of the said industrialist that he has installed in his workplaces the best steam engine available. Later, though, this announcement proves incomplete, because the owner, for whatever reason, has shut off the steam, shut down the engines, and even pulled the belts off of the wheels, while adding enough personnel to render the machines superfluous.

After all, does the magistrate who *in the abstract* is obligated to investigate God's Word in Scripture but *in practice* is not competent to do so, not have to act according to the light of the natural knowledge of God? The only advantage that could lie in this for the freedom of thought, speech, and action of citizens is entirely lost through the highly dubious theory that the magistrate's duty to act according to the Word could come into play at any moment, as soon as

---

[61] See above, pp. 48ff.

public opinion, or, to call things by their name, the ruling party, is able to push its positive viewpoints directly or indirectly onto him.

This opinion is in principle Roman Catholic. The magistrate does not himself know what the truth is, but he comes to know it by a detour, through those who rule over him. A rather dangerous opinion!

We are now drawing conclusions from some data which in our view are highly implausible. For: is it so entirely certain that the magistrate officially *must* do something that he at the same time *cannot* do? So certain that he *cannot* or *may not* do something but still, on penalty of sinning against God and shirking a stern duty, *has* to know or do it, or *had* to have known or done it, or *had to have been able* to know or do it?

Human language has no words the meaning of which is as malleable and at the same time as splintery as *can, may,* and *must*. With these words, one can work wonders in an argumentation. And if one can view the people that must, that can, and that may, in one moment as they are, in another moment in their official capacity, and in a third moment from a certain viewpoint, and makes no distinction between capacity to *know* and capacity to *implement,* one quickly runs into a dead end.

"My hearers!" announced a member of the Boys' Club addressing the group on an extremely important subject, the freedom of the will. "Man has no free will, for if he did, no one would have perished in the Flood!"

But we need not yet ask whether *must* is possible while *can* is not, in view of the fact that in the nature of the case, *cannot* must first be established. Whence does Dr. Kuyper derive the incapacity of the magistrate to know the will of the Lord?

1) From the extent of the investigation. "Such an extensive knowledge of nature, reason, Scripture, and history, such a thorough investigation and extraordinarily clear insight is needed to understand the will of God in every given instance, that one can safely say that this knowledge factually lies beyond the reach of the magistrate." A sad affair. If this is true, we need to revise our concept of revelation. Nature, reason, Scripture, religion and science, an article in the

Confession and a thesis in the back of a doctoral dissertation,[62] all stand on the same level. Our conception of Scripture is then untenable.

If *The Herald* is right, at a minimum it ceases to be the rule for our faith and our practice, because what Dr. Kuyper says here about the magistrate is applicable to everyone and to every action of man. One needs to know everything in order to grasp anything. This changes our consciousness of duty. In the case in question, we do not ourselves have to act according to the light that we have and the degree of knowledge imparted to us, but may postpone devotion to duty until the extensive investigation is completed which *The Herald* hazards.

2) From the fact that not every magistrate has a Bible. "There are thousands upon thousands of government personnel in Asia and Africa who are born and who soon will die without having had the opportunity to see one single chapter of Scripture." Answer: Romans 2: 12ff.

3) From the darkening of human understanding by sin. "Something else than external and formal reading is needed to understand God's will. Or does the Apostle not teach us that 'the natural man does not understand the things of the Spirit of God,' and did not Jesus Himself speak to us in the same manner that 'he who is not born of water and spirit cannot even see the kingdom of God?' or to take an entirely different expression: does Jesus not say that it is the Father's good will to hide these things from the wise and understanding?" Certainly – but *not about that which pertains to the terrain and vocation of the magistrate.* Should we apply the cited texts to the entire Scripture, we would then be able to say in this regard: if the light that God shines in Scripture is darkness, how great is that darkness!

Rome would then be correct in keeping Scripture out of everyone's hands and reserving the interpretation of Scripture to itself. We would have to add to everyone who says to us that he wishes to live according to God's Word: arrange your life, your behavior according to God's Word? Not so fast, my friend! Tell me first: are you converted? And do you have the Spirit...?

---

[62] [A reference to the custom at European universities to include a list of theses in the back of a dissertation, the first of which pertain to the subject matter, the last of which are of more general import.]

How did Dr. Kuyper come to proclaim this doctrine? Human beings are able to communicate their commands to subordinates in understandable language, but when God makes known His will to His servant, He *hides* it!

Results of the Survey

The goal of our provisional investigation, the survey of the terrain, has now been reached. Dr. Kuyper will now speak of the relation of the magistrate to *the church,* something that should only come in the second place, as already stated. Nevertheless, we will only be able to establish the result of our investigation fully when we have shown in this section of our essay what we soon, in various relations, will have to contest.

The main points of disagreement concern:

1) the claim in no. 1171 that the political principle of Article 36, which Dr. Kuyper disputes, is the logical continuation of what Constantine imposed on the church;

2) that in determining the relation between church and magistrate as God wills it, one may not extend his investigation to, or as the writer expresses it, may not take refuge in, the Old Testament;

3) that the New Testament (no. 1173) does not require any specific behavior from the magistracies of the nations towards the church (no. 1174);

4) that the magistrate would have to support the church even with the strong arm if a) the character of the church did not forbid this; b) one did not have to exercise any faith in order accurately to appraise the truthfulness of the gospel that the church brings, and if faith was not a gift of God; c) if one did not have to be born again to see the kingdom of God, so that an unregenerate magistrate is excluded;

5) that even if what is said in a), b), and c) above were not true, the (previously undivided) church having been divided since the Reformation, the impossibility of applying this principle in an irrefutable manner has been demonstrated;

6) to wit, that the magistrate is not authorized to take sides between the instituted churches. Dr. Kuyper argues that even with the best intentions he could

not do so. The Reformation did away with the magisterium, and thus the unity, of the church.

In brief, it was an illusion on the part of the fathers that unity could better be maintained along a different path than was taken by the Roman Catholic church (no. 1186). The Confession was drawn up during a time in which this illusion had not yet been given up (nos. 1185, 1187). With this illusion went the last thing that advocated for the conception of the fathers as put forward in Article 36. The unity of the church, i.e., the authority of the church, which restricts the revelation of life, was exchanged for the freedom of the Christian man.

Thus far Dr. Kuyper.

Of course, we do not agree with him; what is more, he does not agree with himself. In no. 1188, do we not read that our fathers did not have the slightest idea of charging the magistrate with maintaining the nominally Reformed church, but only the Reformed religion? Absolutely true. But is this not a complete refutation of much of what the writer puts forward in this same essay, including much that he had just affirmed, to wit, that Article 36 is the culmination of what Constantine did, in connection with the bit about the illusion regarding the unity of the church?

In general we can say this about Dr. Kuyper's manner of argumentation: it is often incidental, i.e., it has the goal of eliminating opposition on a specific point. This has a great advantage. One is prepared with the argument that is most convincing at that particular moment. For example, in connection with the rationale summarized above, he wished to demonstrate that the proponents of the national church who did not take its confessional character so seriously and thus could embrace a wide range of doctrine, had no right to appeal to Article 36. In the same way, in this case the emphasis is put on the Confession, on religion, as if the church in Dr. Kuyper's essay is not the instituted and divided church. But this does not hinder him from denying this confessional character once and for all when it suits the discussion, thus shortly thereafter.

In no. 1187, the appeal to this article is once again refuted, in yet another manner. Many confessional statements were drafted, as is known, with the goal of gaining the favor the magistrate for the church, and with that favor, the support it desired, or at least the freedom. From this the writer deduces that *Article*

36 does not belong in the Confession. Note that he says this in a specific context. It remains to be seen, however, whether he who presents this argument is also prepared to repudiate the *potestas dogmatica* of the church, and to undermine the scientific foundation of the Free University.[63] For now we leave this out of consideration. There are factors in the history of the ecclesiastical conflict and of the law faculty at the school on the Reformed basis [i.e., the Free University], that lead us to speak less decisively on this point than we otherwise would. For the moment, though, we would rather assume that what is dubious in the above remark, and the use made of it in the essay, is attributable to the writer's manner of argument. Otherwise we encounter here as well a point of difference that runs deep and would require an investigation of its own.

Regardless, we need not languish in uncertainty on this point, for Dr. Kuyper now expresses himself freely. If the magistrate wishes to choose between the existing churches, he will have to determine what the true form of the church is, and what these other groups are that call themselves "church" but are not. Listen: "And now, to those who wish to maintain Article 36 unchanged – and they have no right to any further input as long as they have not given a pertinent and conclusive answer – we pose this question that dominates the entire disagreement: how is the magistrate to determine which of the many churches is the only true one, given that he encounters more than one visible church?"

Will he protect and help the true church and meanwhile "remove all idolatry and false worship" etc.... Shall we complete the sentence for the writer? Perhaps readers here or there have noticed the fallacy that we would rather not have to indicate time and time again.... "If he is to protect the true church and meanwhile remove all idolatry and false worship, then he must be apprised as to whether Luther or Zwingli is right about the doctrine of the Lord's Supper, as well as whether church order is to be maintained by classes, superintendents, boards, or bishops"! Is it not evident how inappropriate, and how much in conflict with the entire conception of our fathers, it is to equate the true church with some denomination? Does Article 36 teach that it is not the Reformed religion, but this or that church form, which is to be considered the mark of the true church?

---

[63] [Namely, the right of public interpretation.]

The subsequent essay, no. 1188, merely contains conclusions deducted from the amusing assumption that the magistrate will have to choose among the denominations, sects, and parties that exist in this country, along with a summary of the difficulties that he would encounter if he had "the high courage" to pursue such a goal in practice. "We draw attention to the difficulty that those who do not share our gravamen to Article 36 must overcome, trusting that will have the high courage to present for evaluation their conceptions in concrete form, for our country at this time, and preferably as a draft constitution proposal."

We knew that Dr. Kuyper was not neutral in the bad sense of the word, that he does not run with the Liberals, and that he is firmly convinced that "those who maintain the Romish (!) unity-idea without the Romish organization" hinder the freedom of the churches and cause damage to all manner of interests (no. 1193, thesis 20). We never doubted this and do not need to summarize this part. It would not bring the discussion any further.

We may therefore proceed to discuss the objections to Article 36, but we take the freedom to place them in the proper context. By doing so, we confront system with system. We thus concisely expound the basic ideas in the program of constitutional reform, which we append here with an eye to the objections put forward in the essays on "church and state."

An Agenda for Constitutional Reform based on Article 36

We acknowledge, with respect to:

1. Sovereignty

a. that God alone is sovereign, Whom both people and magistrate must honor as such;

b. that God has revealed His will in the creation ordinances, in the leading of Providence, in the consciences of men, and quite clearly in His holy Word;

c. that in consequence the legislative and executive power is bound to His will.

2. The civil magistrate

a. that the magistrate rules "by the grace of God," and excepting the guarantees given by the constitution against possible arbitrariness, is also exclusively responsible to God;

b. that *private judgement* regarding Holy Scripture accrues to the magistrate just as it does to every citizen, and that this judgement is tied not only to the conscience of civil servants but to conscience illuminated by *the church's public interpretation* laid down in its Confession, recognized as such by the constitution, and included among the guarantees of the *liberties of the people;*

c. that God has placed the sovereignty in this country in the House of Orange, excepting what results from the just-established principle.

3. The nation

That our nation is a Christian, Protestant, Reformed nation, and that all principled parity between belief and unbelief, between paganism and Christianity, is, in consideration of our history, our popular character, and the demand of God's Word, which is the same for all times and for all peoples, ruled out from the start.

4. The national church

a. That this national character is connected with and is an expression of the national church, the revelation of the body of Christ in this country, as it manifests itself, cleansed of errors, in the *Reformed* church;

b. that in consequence the *public-legal* character of this church is to be recognized under the stipulations contained in the essence of the church, of the Confession, and of the ecclesiastical offices.

5. National institutions

That *all national institutions,* no matter what kind, whether or not directly or indirectly derived from the church or attached to it, apart from the rights of certain citizens or groups of citizens to be delineated later, whether or not manifesting themselves in separate churches, *must demonstrate this Christian, Protestant, Reformed national character,* and therefore must stand in complete opposition to that which, as an expression of so-called neutrality of the civil government, in fact must be viewed as a denial of the first and foremost foundation of the state – subjection to *the revealed will of God.*

6. *The constitution*

That neither the constitution nor the people are above the civil government, but that the constitution describes and delineates the task of the magistrate, and that the people assist the state in the exercise of that task with all possible aid.

7. *Popular representation*

a. That the people have a representation to that end, which propounds its interests to the magistrate, and that the vocation of that representation is not to exercise joint rule but to advance the various interests of the nation in all its segments and have them come into their own;

b. that to that end, the people needs to be represented as purely as possible, and that the better the principle of *sovereignty* (Article 1) is maintained, the less necessary it is to make exclusive conditions for certain groups of the representation.

8. *Jews and Roman Catholics*

a. That, in conflict with the main principle of the constitution now in force, Jews form no part of the Dutch nation, but rather are a nation that enjoy guest status here, and *as such* even have the right to have its own representatives which represent its interests to the magistrate;[64]

b. that, in conflict with that same principle (Article 12), Roman Catholics, by virtue of the confession of their church, recognize an authority that stands over the country's magistrate, over the constitution, and, because of its magisterium, over God's Word, and therefore cannot be permitted to fill influential positions in the state without requisite restrictions;

c. that the system whereby the popular representatives are designated by the majority of citizens with voting rights, leads unavoidably to an unbecoming preponderance of the most numerous over the less numerous groups in the nation;

---

[64] [For their part, many Jews originally did not agree with undistinguished citizenship status – they did not wish to see their separate nationhood dissolved in an undifferentiated mass. See Koenen, *Geschiedenis der Joden in Nederland* [History of the Jews in the Netherlands] (Utrecht: C. van der Post Jr., 1843), pp. 363–366. For himself, Hoedemaker professed to be pro-Semite and pro-Zionist: *The Reformed Church,* no. 581 (23 November 1899).]

that this wrong is not entirely removed by representation of heads of households, and that universal suffrage, under the appearance of doing right by everyone, necessarily prepares the way to the tyranny of the non-propertied over the propertied classes.

9. Freedom of religion

That by virtue of the Protestant principle, no one may be molested on account of his religion. That consequently complete *freedom of religion* is allowed, subject to what is required by public order, what stems from the freedom of others, and what would conflict with the Christian Protestant character of the nation and its public institutions.

10. Christian character of the civil government

While complete freedom of religion is guaranteed to every citizen individually, and can and must be allowed by the magistrate to groups of citizens when the documentation provided to that end shows that what presents itself as religion does not extend to the overthrow of the foundations of the Christian state, and while even dispensation from the satisfaction of certain legal stipulations can be granted by the magistrate out of respect for religious objections of conscience; it, that is, the civil government, is bound in its doings to the Confession of the national church, and it is its duty to consult this church in its lawful assemblies or, if the case entails this, the university professors of this church, as experts regarding the principles that are to be derived from these principles, in order to be informed by theological counsel where appropriate; in such a way, nevertheless, that the magistrate remains entirely free in his application of these principles to legislation and the country's administration, so that in this sense church and state remain entirely separate, i.e., each remains on its own designated terrain.

11. The oath

The magistrate has the right to require the oath, to wit, the oath according to Christian notions, and to bind to the swearing of this oath the offices and activity as popular representatives.

12. The day of rest

That he is obligated to honor the Christian day of rest and to maintain it is far as possible, not only from a social point of view but out of respect for God's commandment.

13. Morality

That he may not act as accomplice for what is forbidden in God's Word, but must oppose all injustice on public terrain and must punish this to the degree that it is in conflict with Christian notions of morality, i.e., what God's law and Word prescribes for man in his public actions.

This is true in particular for gaming (the lottery), for that which brutalizes man (drunkenness, opium trade) and public decency (whoremongering, propaganda for the two-child system, Mormonism [i.e., polygamy], etc.).

14. Unbelief

That paganism may not be tolerated in public life and may not be permitted in public.

15. Public health

That the magistrate may not permit the practice of what science prescribes as good and necessary for the people and in particular for the health of the people, but which violates religious conviction, namely in the persons who by virtue of Christian notions object to those prescriptions (vaccination).

16. The sword of justice

That he act as avenger for the punishment of evildoers, and consequently must be on the lookout for principles in penal law or in adjudication that conflict with the principle here expressed, such as e.g. the principle that punishment exclusively serves to protect and improve, or the opinion that reasonable, moral, freely acting beings are unaccountable if under the influence of certain instincts or certain influences which stand in the power of man (such as crimes committed while drunk, or attributable to inherited punishable inclinations such as kleptomania, etc.).

17. Primary and higher education

That the vocation of the magistrate with regard to education is not to be derived from state interest, especially not from the fact that the state needs capable civil servants and well-educated citizens, nor from the national interest, i.e., the notion of its functions, by which all higher communal interests such as art, science, education, religion, are turned into its domain, but from the principle that, with regard to science, art, religion, the church, it enable the citizens – and with regard to education, the parents – to fulfill their duties, whereby in the case of education it has the vocation to stand up for under-age children vis-à-vis parents.

This entails:

a. that he ensure sufficient primary education all across the country;

b. that he as far as possible leave the establishment and maintenance of schools to private entities, and consequently support this private initiative;

c. that, where this initiative is not taken, he establish schools under school boards chosen by parents;

d. that sufficient primary education is only given where guarantees are in place to ensure that the Christian element in education is not lacking;

e. that oversight of this be vested in the consistory of the congregation, with the understanding that it may either leave Bible instruction to the educator or provide it itself;

f. that he allow parents to decide whether their children will participate in this education or not;

g. that he provide public higher education under the following restrictions:

1. the appointment of professors be entrusted to separate commissions for the various faculties, in which men sit who may be considered to represent the sciences which are given at the university or universities; the appointment of this commission or this curatorium is entrusted, as far as the theological faculty is concerned, to the church;

2. the number and appointment of subjects and chairs in this faculty is determined by the church, or at least according to advice provided by the church.

3. Groups of citizens are free, under the requisite restrictions, with regard to the scientific content of teachers and that which pertains to a sufficient plan of instruction, to set up parallel faculties or chairs in connection with the university in order to provide for their religious and ecclesiastical needs.

2. EVALUATION

In his Stone Lectures presented in Princeton in the United States of America in 1898, Dr. Kuyper characterizes the sentiment that the country's government would be obliged to remove false religion as "the fatal after-effect of a system, grey with age, which Calvinism found in existence, under which it had grown up, and from which it had not yet been able entirely to liberate itself."[65]

This statement happens to contradict a well-known article in our Confession, to which we have repeatedly made reference. We thought this was frankly recognized in the statement tabled at the church assembly in Middelburg. Even so, the Stone Lectures show that we were mistaken – that is, if "Calvinistic" and "Reformed" have roughly the same meaning.

Speaking of "Calvinism and Politics," Dr. Kuyper expressly states, "In order to shield myself from this undesirable suspicion (to wit, that he opposes Calvinism), I advance the rule—that a system is not known in what it has in common with other preceding systems; but that it is distinguished by that in which it differs from those preceding systems."[66]

The opinion that the government is called to remove false religion is something that Calvinism has in common with other and earlier systems. The deduction is thus plain: one may reject this opinion without ceasing to be a good Calvinist.

Here we confront an extremely curious rule that causes us to doubt something we thought we were certain of, which allows Dr. Kuyper to rescind something that he so recently expressed in public in such a solemn manner. What sort of Calvinism is this, we might ask, by which, with the help of the above-mentioned rule, an operation can take place whereby someone who presents himself as an opponent and repudiator of a rather important element of our

---

[65] *Lectures on Calvinism,* p. 100.
[66] *Ibid.*

Confession, is now able to elevate – by way of logic – his orthodoxy above all doubt?

In the first place, it is certain that this rule is not applicable to our Confession, because that Confession contains all manner of general Christian elements. This lies in the nature of the case. The church did not first arise during the Synod of Dort, or even the Reformation. Nor does its history date from Pentecost. It dates from Paradise. If we, in the footsteps of Paul in ch. 4 of his letter to the Ephesians, imagine the church as a body that grows "unto a perfect man," and compare the Confession to a human face, then we can say that the fresh face of the boy has become more lined and more full of character, but we cannot separate what has changed in it from what is unchanged. The continuity of life is not interrupted; identity is preserved.

We can even say that the child "is the father of the man," that the man must become "as a little child" (Mark 10: 15), or, what Coleridge characterized as the most outstanding thing we can honor in someone, that he "remained a child." We can thus safely assume that the rule established by Dr. Kuyper cannot be applied to the Confession of the church.

The apostle Paul taught that Abraham was saved by the same faith as that which saves us in the New Testament. And the Reformers included the three credal statements of the catholic Christian church among the Forms of Unity as the expression of the faith of Protestants, alongside the articles from the time after the Reformation.

We may conclude from this that Dr. Kuyper's language is far from benign. Why does he prefer to use the terms "Calvinist" and "Calvinism" to designate his and his followers' viewpoints regarding politics? Why does he reserve the designation "Reformed" for the church and a part of its theology? Not because Calvin deviated from the principle expressed in Article 36 of our Confession regarding the vocation of the government respecting idolatry and false religion. Not because (excluding the republican form of government, which the Reformer *found* in Geneva, for he did not bring it there) anything that could serve as a point of contact with the opinions expressed by Dr. Kuyper and his followers can be found in his system. But because the theological-philosophical system that goes by the name of Calvinism offers a framework for his notions, as long as he may express what we heard him say: Calvin taught things that *conflicted with his own principle.* One step farther and we are confronted with the thesis: he who combats Calvin is the best Calvinist, because he improves on him!

But we do not need to consult Calvin's *Institutes* to discover something to which Dr. Kuyper's principle might apply, because the only thing to which he himself refers is not relevant here. He found something in Calvin with which he is even less in agreement, and which he combats. After having claimed, as we saw, that the problematic clause in Article 36 is an error with which Calvin was also saddled, he continues in this fashion:

> If I wish to know what derives from Calvinism's own principle, then the question must be posed entirely differently. In that case it must be realized and recognized that the system by which deviations in matters of religion are brought under the jurisdiction of the civil magistrate, stems directly from the conviction that the church of Christ on earth can only manifest itself in one form and as one institute. This one church alone was the church of Christ, and everything that deviated from it was considered to be hostile to the one true church. Therefore, the government did not have to decide, nor even to approve. There was only one church of Christ on earth, and it had to protect that one conceivable church from schism, heresy, and sect.

Allow us to refresh the readers' memory. Dr. Kuyper claimed that a system is not known from that which it has in common with others. He was therefore going to show us something specific to Calvinism with which he was in agreement, something to demonstrate that he might call himself a Calvinist ... and he refers to Calvin's church concept, with which *he is even less in agreement!* We will provide the evidence that he has not presented the facts accurately here. Nevertheless, assuming them to be accurate, then precisely the opposite would follow from Dr. Kuyper's pronouncement than that which he wished to demonstrate.

Be that as it may, we leave the logic of this to Dr. Kuyper's account and affirm again that his language is anything but benign. It is rooted in the dualism between his political theory and his theology. It allows him to lodge all manner of objections to the Confession without being called to account. It betrays misunderstanding of both the Confession and Holy Scripture, but in that Scripture, of the chief principle of Protestantism.

When for example he says in the Stone Lectures that "The duty of the government to extirpate every form of false religion and idolatry ... dates from Constantine the Great, and was the reaction against the horrible persecutions which his pagan predecessors on the imperial throne had inflicted upon the sect of the Nazarene,"[67] he is saying that the Christians, having become the ruling party in government, copied the persecution of heretics from their heathen predecessors, and the Protestants in turn copied it from the Roman Catholics. But he forgets entirely that the principles according to which these three groups acted had nothing in common. Here the proverb is entirely apropos, that when two say the same thing, it is not necessarily the same. The author must not have a very high opinion of his readership if he runs together such heterogenous things in this manner.[68]

But in so speaking he has at the same time done something which is even more fraught with danger.

---

[67] *Ibid.*

[68] Was pagan Rome not an example of religious toleration? Was it not on the same level as the modern state in this regard? Do Christians then not have to fear any conflict with the state if they, like their forebears from the post-apostolic period, come into conflict with the civil laws? Religion was interwoven with public life in all manner of ways in the Roman state, while the modern state has little to nothing of this. But this does not affect the principle. Civil law must be obeyed. Might we not say with some justification that the most liberal government today applies the principle of Article 36 in an area in which it is important to it to intervene in the lives and activities of citizens, to wit, morality and public health? Has one forgotten how the Salvation Army and Mormonism were dealt with in Switzerland? If so, then allow me to point out what occurs in the Netherlands, to wit, the ostracism of Christ's church, to the degree that this can occur by human action from outside. The modern state does not tolerate the church on its [i.e., the public] terrain. It only knows of [private] clubs, societies, and foundations, and should one desire recognition before the law, it must come in these forms. Speaking of removal, it is not possible to suppress a moral person more effectively than our constitution does.

Dr. Kuyper encroaches on the Confession in its *essence,* when he characterizes it as the echo of public opinion rather than the summary of Holy Scripture (*repetitio Sacrae Scripturae*). The truth of a conviction, says our Confession, is not demonstrated by its antiquity, nor by its universality, and least of all by its derivation from an unbroken succession of ordained teachers. Only agreement with Holy Scripture demonstrates truthfulness. The Reformed church is distinguished from the Lutheran precisely in its demand that doctrine and practice not merely not be in conflict with Scripture, but that they be derived from it. If the Confession is in error, then it must be a consequence of the improper interpretation of Scripture.

We have now returned to the question: what is Dr. Kuyper's position vis-à-vis Scripture, Confession, and the church, when we consider these in mutual connection? By now we have given up the hope, arising from or awakened by the submission of the oft referred-to statement at the assembly in Middelburg, that we would discover the grounds upon which the deviation from Article 36 is based, as derived from Holy Scripture. We are continually brought back to this question, to which we can give no answer, unless – and we do this grudgingly – we go on the attack.

Grudgingly?

To the degree that it is necessary to bring the affair to a proper conclusion, quite the opposite. Besides what we openly must dispute in Dr. Kuyper's way of thinking because we see clear Romish tendencies therein, we also see indications that he combats a caricature of what the Reformed Confession says on this point, in order to facilitate arriving at a different understanding.

And now to business.

The Role of Scripture in Kuyper's System

We ask in the first place: what is the place that Holy Scripture occupies in the system that Dr. Kuyper gladly calls "Calvinism"? And we answer, it betrays a misunderstanding

1) of Scripture's normative authority.

The normative character of Holy Scripture

In his *Tract on the Ecclesiastical Power,*[69] Voetius responds to the question regarding whether the ecclesiastical power is vested in the magistrate or the church and its ministers; and he asserts that his answer is entirely independent of circumstances of period of time, more specifically favor or lack thereof on the part of the magistrate.

> We expressed literally the same thing when the magistrate was antagonistic to the church and the truth. We now bear witness that the Lord has seen fit to have the church find favor in the eyes of the civil magistrate since the year 1618. We will continue to say it even if the favor of today changes to disfavor tomorrow. Hilarius accused those contemporaries who did not remain the same, and did not stay true to their principle, that they had a faith in the times and not in the gospels. May the same not be said of us.

Thus spoke Voetius. This is everyone's position who asks not for what yields advantage, but only for what God commands in His Word. This was our fathers' position when they saw and expressed the truth that, misused by erring men, could cost them property and life. They put, as it were, the sword into the hands of the civil government to kill them, but remained faithful to the principle that the origin and vocation of civil government is independent of the goal that it pursues, the religion it confesses, the country in which it resides.

Rather lose everything than weaken the demand of God's holy law for temporal advantage! "For you the same thing is good today, evil tomorrow; what is

---

[69] [*Schriftmatige en redenkundige verhandeling over de kerkelyke macht: waer in grondig betoogt wordt, dat deselve niet aen de politike overheit, maer aen de kerke en haere dienaeren toekomt* [Scriptural and philosophical tract of the ecclesiastical power: in which it is thoroughly demonstrated that this power does not appertain to the political government but to the church and its ministers] (Rotterdam: Hendrik van Pelt & Adrianus Douci, 1756).]

truth on this side of the Pyrenees is a lie on the other!" hoots Pascal at the Jesuits in his *Provincial Letters*. This could not remotely be said of our fathers.

But we would not dare to make the same claim for those who, to use Dr. Kuyper's expression in the Stone Lectures, "pick up the gauntlet for Calvinism."[70] What it was that motivated the signers of the Middelburg statement to consider the question of principle regarding the vocation of the civil government, is something we can only surmise. A few years ago, Dr. Kuyper considered the question as to whether Article 36 conformed to God's Word, to be of no practical significance whatsoever. "If it were true that our people consisted of faithful Calvinists," we heard him say,[71] "and among the 4½ million Dutchmen there were at most 100,000 dissenters, we might consider a 'do-over,' although taking into account what we see in Spain and Portugal, we would certainly counsel against it." A note in passing: What do Spain and Portugal, in which Roman Catholic principles are applied in state law, have to do with the application of Reformed principles? Or is Dr. Kuyper not aware of the distinction between the two? This would explain his opposition to Article 36. We would then also understand what he wrote in the same connection, "Reformed Christians in the land would not in the least desire the government to again officially confess the Reformed religion." This is to be expected of Reformed Christians who travel to Spain and Portugal to see Reformed-Calvinistic principles put into practice.

Likewise when he wrote: "Rightly did these Reformed, then, see that there was absolutely no hurry to revise what presented itself in their Confession regarding the relation between church and state." Why not? Because it is like the architect who, following his own insight, deviates from the specification. He does not ask for a new specification, for he has no intention of adhering to it. Things work out just as well without specification and blueprint!

But herein lies the error that we now point out, to wit, not the public challenging, not the fundamental rejection, but the *de facto* negation of the normative authority of Holy Scripture. In certain specific areas, one simply does not take God's Word into account any more as rule for faith and practice. The

---

[70] *Lectures on Calvinism,* p. 99.

[71] *The Herald,* January 22nd, 1892.

temptation not to is extreme, by the way, especially when one wishes to get things done in a church and among a people for which this rule is not required. After all, we have to conform to the state of affairs!

Hence, in order to avoid misunderstanding, let us be clear that respect for the normative authority of Holy Scripture does not keep us from taking existing, abnormal reality into account; instead, it requires it. The question is only whether we will abandon the truth, the ideal, the requirement of God's holy will, the goal and destination. Everyone always has to take reality into account, otherwise he is a dreamer and becomes false. But he who yields the truth in favor of reality, chooses opportunity as his guide.

To a degree, we do have to take reality into account. A sailor does not always sail in a straight line. He tacks, avoids the shoals, yields to a ship or an iceberg, but his goal is fixed, and all the while it determines his course; he does not float along with the current, nor does he sail wherever the wind blows, not knowing where he will end up. It is impossible to say *a priori* the degree to which Christian prudence should extend in a given situation.

Our fathers discussed this question with their customary scrupulousness and exhaustiveness under the heading, "regarding toleration." But what holds for us is "that I renounce and forsake all creatures, rather than commit even the least thing contrary to his will."[72]

The deviation regarding the normative authority of Holy Scripture is rooted, though, in an error regarding

2) the perspicuity of Scripture (the *perspicuitas Sacrae Scripturae*).

The perspicuity of Holy Scripture

Dr. Kuyper used to teach that "the civil government stands outside the terrain of revealed religion and, in terms of capacity, possesses natural but not directly supernatural knowledge of God." Furthermore, that the government has "no decisive answer" regarding the question, "what duties the gospel imposes upon the people" in view of the fact that "the gospel lies outside its sphere and beyond its reach, and it lacks the authorization to choose among the diverging answers given by other (churches) to this question."[73]

---

[72] Heidelberg Catechism, 34th Sunday. *Three Forms of Unity*, p. 14.

[73] *Our Program*, §56.

The provenance of this, in our view perilous error appears from the following statement, made in the same context: "The non-confessing government could only take the revealed knowledge of God as guideline for its action if a supernatural organ existed to determine with absolute certainty what the revealed will of God demands in every given case."[74]

Besides the objections that are appropriate in our context against the system proposed in these citations in *Our Program,* the following objection can be lodged. The *confessing* civil government may therefore take the revealed knowledge of God as guideline for its action.... A dangerous doctrine, if this confession is that of the Roman church.

A Reformed person says: regardless of whether one is pagan, Jew, Roman Catholic, or Reformed, you have the same vocation derived from the Scriptural concept of your office, and are illuminated with more or less clarity by the same truth. But the Romanist believes that a supernatural organ to expound Scripture does indeed exist. If "the confessing civil government" believes this, then, according to Dr. Kuyper, it may also apply it.

Is it not apparent what a principle of tyranny is contained within this thesis which we contest? It is purely Romish. This teaching strikes the doctrine of the perspicuity of Holy Scripture in its aorta. We now hear him say, "It remains the duty of the civil magistrate to decide and act in agreement with the revealed will of God" but at the same time he assures us that this won't do, in view of the fact that "for practical action, it is not enough that the will of God be revealed in general, because that will, in order for one to act in terms of it, must be personally revealed" and it is not enough for this personal revelation that a copy of God's Word lies within our reach, "because their eyes must spiritually be opened to understand that Word."[75]

From this it appears that the discrepancy noted above is not isolated, but goes together with the viewpoint of common as opposed to particular grace, which is not Protestant but really is Romish (see pp. 45f. above), and with the

---

[74] *Ibid.,* §51 [see n. 55].

[75] *The Herald,* nos. 1163 and 1165. See p. 52 above.

no less Romish concept regarding the interpretation of Holy Scripture. *Our Program* speaks of "a supernatural organ" – the church – while the latest articles in *The Herald* speak of "a supernatural illumination."

Dr. Kuyper withholds this book from the civil government for the same reason that the Roman church withholds it from the people.[76] His reasoning is as follows: "Whoever does not believe is hostile to the gospel in his heart. Being enemies of God, we are drawn to the gospel by the divine power. Born blind, our eyes are opened by God. And as long as that grace has not occurred, we cannot take a single step. A civil magistrate who is not born of water and spirit, cannot see the kingdom of God," etc. In another connection in which he develops the same thought, he reminds us "that the natural man does not comprehend the things of the Spirit" (1 Cor. 2: 14); "this pertains to those who do not understand the hidden things of the kingdom of heaven" (Luke 8: 10), etc.

This concept is not new. It was recommended both by the sects who took supernatural illumination individually, and by the Romish, who bound it to the church, and was combatted in both forms by the fathers.

Dr. Kuyper's error, as we shall soon demonstrate, lies in his arbitrary determination of the boundaries between the natural and revealed knowledge of God, common and particular grace, etc., in connection with his church concept, which likewise is purely Romish. Our divines were wont to accept "a twofold beholding of God—a *natural* and a *spiritual*.... The *natural* beholding of God is practiced by the unconverted; the *spiritual* beholding of God by those who are true recipients of grace, have truly been regenerated, and truly believe.... The *natural* beholding of God occurs by the light of nature and the external illumination of the Word, by one's own spirit, imagination, and mental powers, and by the drawing of rational conclusions ..." etc.[77] "God favors some with general

---

[76] Robert Bellarmine, *De Verbo Dei* [Of the Word of God] liber III. 19, in *Opera Omnia*, tomus primus; cf. Hodge, *Systematic Theology*, I, pp. 183ff.

[77] Brakel, *A Christian's Reasonable Service*, vol 2, p. 674.

enlightenment whereby they are able to perceive the glory and preciousness of divine truths."[78]

They further made a distinction between the natural-historical, grammatical-logical, dogmatic, and spiritual meaning of the Word. The same writer answered the question as to whether Scripture was difficult to understand, in this manner: "a writer is flawed if he cannot write in an intelligible manner. The more plain and clear his presentation of matters is, enabling the reader to discern the very marrow of the issue at hand, the more learned he is."[79] Of course this is not to deny "that some matters are beyond human comprehension," that "All men are not capable of understanding Scripture from a spiritual perspective."[80]

To the objection derived from the Scripture verses cited by Dr. Kuyper, à Brakel answered, "We readily admit that man needs to be enlightened by God's Spirit before he can understand Scripture in its spiritual sense."[81]

But we believe, as did our fathers, that the Word of God is a lamp unto our feet and a light unto our path, that in that light we also see the things of natural life, and on that basis demand a school with the Bible and proclaim that Holy Scripture is the principle of all true science.

The civil government, God's servant, finds the revelation of God's holy will in that Scripture. On that basis, Groen van Prinsterer taught that "the state, i.e., the organic whole of all the nation's interests, cannot be built upon an atheistic or pantheistic system, but only on the authority and will of Jesus Christ, the Head of the church and ruler of the kings of the earth." Upon that basis, the States of 1618 "let all kings and princes know that the foundation of the Republic was ... the true religion." On that basis we now repeat what Groen reminded us, that "religion not only was a desirable attitude of citizens but the foundation of legislation and the administration of justice."[82]

---

[78] *Ibid.,* vol. 1, p. 50.

[79] *Ibid.,* p. 51.

[80] *Ibid.,* p. 49.

[81] *Ibid.,* p. 53.

[82] [Source unmentioned.]

This would possibly be otherwise if one could say that religion, the doctrine of faith and morals, and philosophy had no influence whatsoever on the nature of legislation and public policy. The question could then be reduced to what Dr. Kuyper posed: what is the true relation of church and state? But only as long as one equates Holy Scripture with the gospel, the way he repeatedly does in his essay. In that case, one in fact robs Holy Scripture of authority in matters concerning public power and the public life of the people. But now that it has become clear that the rights and duties of prince and people, the vocation of husband, wife, and child, the rich and the poor, the propertied and the laborer, all must be determined either according to and from out of the Word, or from reason, it does not help at all to put Holy Scripture to one side, in or with the Confession.

One is then again confronted with the same question: what is it that determines civil government in its activity? Does it maintain its own system, a sort of state religion and state morality? Does it allow itself to be led by the urgencies of the moment rather than proceed in a scientific manner? In the former case, we get a repetition of pagan Rome, while in the latter it becomes a mere instrument for the ends of the most conniving and inventive political party.

The claim that God bound the civil government to His Word and will, but that the same government is incapable of understanding that Word of God, is a violation of God's honor.

But in the denial of the *perspicuitas Sacra Scripturæ* lies the denial of

3. its sufficiency.

The sufficiency of Holy Scripture

The words "common" and "particular grace" have a familiar ring. The distinction is part and parcel of the omnipotent pleasure of God, by which He – although doing justice to one and all, even the reprobate, and not leaving Himself without witness to anyone, and although His grace and mercy bring near His covenant and the gospel, so that no one may claim "I did not know" or "grace was not within my reach" – grants the grace of regeneration and saving faith "to whom He will."

What, then, are we to understand by that "common grace" [Gemeene Gratie], about which we have been able to read for months on end in *The Herald?* And what is it supposed to mean when one reads in this weekly paper that the civil government acts by the light of *common grace* [gemeene gratie] and the church is the institute of *particular grace* [particuliere gratie]?[83] In what relation does this grace stand to the general and special knowledge of God, general and special revelation, common and particular grace [genade]? One finds here an opposition which the Reformers did not accept, because it is at bottom Anabaptist; the sharp contradiction between nature and grace [genade], the kingdom of God and the kingdom of the world.

According to this viewpoint, the church becomes a kingdom. The expression, Christ the Head of the church, is replaced by Christ the King of His church, not to indicate that Christ rules by His Word and Spirit, but inseparably from the viewpoint of the church as institute. The Bible is not the lawbook of the nation, the light of which the nations speak in Isaiah ch. 1 when they say, "Come let us walk in the light of the Lord!" but something too precious for anyone, something so purely spiritual that there is no use for it unless one is illuminated in supernatural fashion.

This not only infringes on the authority and the perspicuity, but also, as we said, the sufficiency of Holy Scripture. In the second chapter of Groen van Prinsterer's standard work, *Unbelief and Revolution,* he explains the value which must be attached to Holy Scripture in a system which might with any credibility call itself anti-revolutionary. The chapter is entitled "Science against the State Law of the Revolution."[84] We read in the opening paragraphs the following:

> If we were to put together an anti-revolutionary library, the Bible would be the book par excellence, as it is in every library. The new wisdom, when it does not utterly reject revelation, is of the opinion that its statements are not applicable, at least in matters of state law. We, on the other hand (without, as some have done, seeking there an encyclopedia of the sciences) claim that Holy Scripture contains the foundations for everything that concerns law and morality for both peoples and individuals; but I speak of an honest and prayerful investigation,

---

[83] *The Herald,* nos. 1142 and 1147, etc.

[84] [This, the original chapter title, differs from Van Dyke's translation, which has "The Wisdom of the Ages."]

upon which a blessing is promised. The Bible is the infallible touchstone of the truth.

Our unconditional subjection to God's Word has always been the guarantee of dutiful obedience and dutiful resistance, of order and freedom... It is written! That is the axe with which every root of revolutionary theory is cut off.

Put alongside this the series of issues of *The Herald* in which Dr. Kuyper indicates the place that the Bible takes in his system, and it will dawn on you while you read them that you are moving within an entirely different thought-world.

You learn from this how wrong "the common understanding is, as if the government derives the light for its task from the Bible." It is made clear to you that "Scripture is not a book of recipes for which an index could be drawn up to find a ready answer to every question that crops up." And, after having attacked various and sundry standpoints that no one is defending, and defending what no one is attacking, you hear that for most people the Bible is a closed book. A closed book, either because they do not possess it, or because they do not understand it, or because those who are considered to understand it are divided amongst themselves, so that the poor magistrate is like Buridan's ass, stuck between two equidistant bunches of hay, standing immobile because he does not know which to choose.

To what was said first, he adds that the civil government is a real government even though it does not have the Bible; also, that the systems of state law that arose outside of Scripture were so outstanding and had so much of value.

About the second remark, he reminds us that

the Kaffir king in Africa does not understand much of Revelation... in view of the fact that such an expansive knowledge, such a thoroughgoing investigation and such exceptionally clear insight is needed to understand the will of God from nature, reason, Scripture, and history, that most people become dismayed by investigation of Scripture alone.

In fact, only principles applicable in specific instances can be derived from Scripture, and then only after extensive investigation.

Therefore, it is not difficult to demonstrate that a subject must obey his ruler, but it is not easy to determine whether he must honor Lord Roberts or President Steyn.[85]

Our fathers, if they could get ahold of Dr. Kuyper, would have a word with him about the *sufficientia Sacrae Scripturae,* the sufficiency of Holy Scripture. The Roman Catholics of their day were of the opinion that Scripture was not up to the task of serving as guide for ruler and subject, the man of science and of practice. Tradition, the church, philosophy the handmaid of theology, must come to its assistance.[86] And in opposition to those Roman Catholics, they maintained that everything that was necessary to know, not only for salvation, but also to understand nature, man, and life, both in this world and the coming one, could be found in Scripture. As is well-known, this did not mean that they thought they could find a revealed physics or chemistry, doctrine of state and morality in Holy Scripture, but that they derived the basic concepts which rule these sciences from Scripture, and were absolutely convinced that those who do not take Scripture into account could only achieve a certain scholarly ignorance.

The light leaves untouched the things it enables us to see. But it is the indispensable condition for every independent, sufficient, and satisfactory investigation.

We draw no distinction here between the sciences amongst themselves. There are those that derive the entirety of their subject matter from Scripture, and there are those that do so from nature, with or without microscope or telescope. There are also those, and among these we include state law, that must discover their basic concepts and principles from Scripture, or chiefly from Scripture, because the knowledge of rights and duties is derived from the Word. But it is Scripture which designates the ruling principle by which the entire system is formed.

---

[85] *The Herald,* nos. 1147, 1151, etc. [Lord Roberts: Field Marshal Frederick Sleigh Roberts, 1st Earl Roberts, commander-in-chief of the British Army in the Second Boer War. President Steyn: Martinus Theunis Steyn, President of the Orange Free State during the Second Boer War.]

[86] William Ames (Amesius), *Bellarminus enervatus,* I ch. 6.

In this light we see light.

How did Groen come to attach such a high value, and more specifically, the principle of all science, to that Word of God, as the passage in ch. 2 of *Unbelief and Revolution* indicates? Because he used a different standard than Dr. Kuyper did above, when Kuyper said he was reminding his readers that Scripture does not indicate to us who the legitimate government is at any given time. Groen knew that the Revolution had shifted the center of gravity of all of life and all knowledge, and that all errors in modern times were branches of the same chief error. Read, e.g., what he wrote about Haller: "Haller realized that the entire composition of more recent legal science rested on one untrue presupposition. The opinion, namely, that the state arose by human consent, which put an end to the state of nature." One single incorrect assumption, in this example, was thus the formative principle of this science, or rather of the reigning systems in this area of science.

One may then certainly attribute a transformative, likewise reforming, influence to one correct assumption! But where does one derive this correct assumption? From the Bible, and more specifically, what this Bible makes known about God and man, sin and redemption.

Dr. Kuyper would not contradict this. On the contrary, we find the same thought developed in outstanding fashion in his latest contributions on "Church and State" in *The Herald*. In no. 1166, for instance, we read: "a doctrine of state that is not based on a proper psychology and on a proper knowledge of man generally, cannot lead to the desired result." Even more clearly in the following excerpt from the same issue: "Every science must be erected from principles, and the acceptance of Holy Scripture as the highest authority is such a deeply intrusive principle that it dominates the entirety of the structure of state law."

The difference between us arises with the questions: 1) are those principles to be derived solely from Scripture, or also from the broad circle of God's revelation in nature? And 2) by whom, along what path, and with what tools does this labor take place?

Dr. Kuyper's theory entails that science joined to Reformed principles functions here by setting the church and the Confession to one side. With this, as we said above, he infringes on the sufficiency of Holy Scripture. Scripture is sufficient because it contains everything that anyone needs to know God's will sufficiently for every area of life.

Dr. Kuyper says that the government is bound to God's will, but that it is so difficult to know that will in a given circumstance because it requires so much study. To this we answer: Scripture is the light by which we see things. Is the light insufficient because we do not find any coal or diamonds, tulips or firs in it? Certainly not. Instead, we see in the visible creation the precious stones and plants that otherwise we would not see.

Scripture does not replace nature, but offers us the key to unravel it. It does so in this manner: we find in Scripture the revelation of God's will, we express it in a confession, we view the world of temporal things – the dismaying plethora of phenomena in every area – in the light of the faith conviction expressed in this confession, and then arrive at the discovery of the unity that Plato in his *Philebus* makes into the objective of all knowledge;[87] but we likewise find that it corresponds with that which we found in Scripture from the outset.

---

[87] ["A gift of heaven, which, as I conceive, the gods tossed among men by the hands of a new Prometheus, and therewith a blaze of light; and the ancients, who were our betters and nearer the gods than we are, handed down the tradition, that whatever things are said to be are composed of one and many, and have the finite, and infinite implanted in them: seeing, then, that such is the order of the world, we too ought in every enquiry to begin by laying down one idea of that which is the subject of enquiry; this unity we shall find in everything. Having found it, we may next proceed to look for two, if there be two, or, if not, then for three or some other number, subdividing each of these units, until at last the unity with which we began is seen not only to be one and many and infinite, but also a definite number; the infinite must not be suffered to approach the many until the entire number of the species intermediate between unity and infinity has been discovered–then, and not till then, we may, rest from division, and without further troubling ourselves about the endless individuals may allow them to drop into infinity. This, as I was saying, is the way of considering and learning and teaching one another, which the gods have handed down to us. But the wise men of our time are either too quick or too slow, in conceiving plurality in unity. Having no method, they

Yet other deviations are contained in the just-indicated error.

The Root of the Deviations

In the first place, we come up against what seems to us to be a gross error – Dr. Kuyper's viewpoint regarding

4) common grace.

Common grace

"There are," holds Dr. Kuyper, "two spheres within which grace works: one which is general and valid for every person, the other which is particular and only of good effect for those who die in Jesus." To what end does common grace serve? "It extends, in opposition to sin, to make human life on earth possible."[88] And particular grace? "It begins with saved persons and their life together in the church of God." Rome separates church and world in this manner, and the Anabaptists, who in this sense live from one and the same basic principle (the kingdom of God visible in the church) restrict the sphere of particular grace to the church.

If one doubted whether Dr. Kuyper intended this, the following citations make his intention quite clear. "In these spheres there are two institutes in which their character is expressed, the institutional church and the instituted state.... They are of entirely different natures.... Common grace finds its intended and direct embodiment in the civil state."

We have already noted that the language that the writer of these *Herald* articles uses deviates from the standardized terminology of our divines.[89] We now

---

make their one and many anyhow, and from unity pass at once to infinity; the intermediate steps never occur to them. And this, I repeat, is what makes the difference between the mere art of disputation and true dialectic." *Parmenides. Theaetetus. Sophist. Statesman. Philebus,* trans. Benjamin Jowett (Oxford: Clarendon Press, 1892), pp. 581–582.]

[88] *The Herald,* nos. 1142, 1146, and 1154.

[89] Above, p. 46.

note that behind this language lurks a difference of principle that immediately becomes evident when we consult those divines.

For instance, compare what Kuyper writes with à Marck, who makes a distinction between inward and outward grace. Everyone who hears the gospel partakes of outward grace, which is called this because it furnishes the means of grace. Inward grace makes the heart receptive to those means, and applies them. From this, one sees that outward grace operates in the sphere or terrain that Dr. Kuyper assigns to particular grace. "This grace," writes de Moor in his commentary on à Marck,[90] "is therefore called common grace because it accords with the external call and does not necessarily lead to salvation."

But the difference lies not only in language per se. A divine may maintain his own terminology and categorization as long as it does not lead to misunderstanding. Nor does the difference lie in the question as to whether the civil government has a different sphere of operation than the church, or what its own vocation is on shared terrain. The views diverge already with the indication of the goal of common grace, namely, to make human life possible in a sinful world.

Is *this* the intention for which God furnishes the means of grace to the lost as well? Dr. Kuyper attaches exceptionally high value to the distinction in grace that he seeks to introduce. "False concepts," he says, "with regard to the civil state, which have made headway among Christians as well, are largely due to the horrendous and extreme unfamiliarity with the essence of common grace."

But it might turn out that this ignorance, if it could speak like the evil spirit in Acts ch. 19, falling upon this common grace, would say "I know common grace, and saving grace too, but you, who are you?"

As if, as often as the Holy Spirit exercises His general influence in the world, the Word and the church were not the organs of the Spirit there as well! As if the hostility engendered by God between the serpent and the woman in

---

[90] Bernardinus de Moor, *Commentarius Perpetuus in Johannes Marckii Compendium Theologiae Christianae Didactico-Elenchticum,* vol. I, ch. IV. § XLII. [English translation: *Bernardinus de Moor's Continuous commentary of Johannes Marckius' Didactico-Elenctic compendium of Christian theology,* vol. 1, trans. Steven Dilday (Culpeper, Virginia : L & G Reformation Translation Center, 2014).]

Paradise, i.e., the grace that hinders man from making peace with Satan, were not the commencement and condition of the work of particular grace!

Yet the conception that we now contest is inseparable from a misconception regarding

5) the natural knowledge of God.

The natural knowledge of God...

This would be immediately evident if Dr. Kuyper's peculiar language did not obscure it. "The civil government stands on the terrain of common [gemeene] grace and receives its light from that common [algemeene] grace." Our Confession, as is known, speaks of two sorts of light, one illuminating us from nature, the other from Scripture. Of which light does the writer speak in the *Herald* articles? He passes over this in silence, but the intention is to make special revelation into an organ of particular grace. This is apparent from the entire discourse.

"Common grace introduces nothing new, no new power, but serves to maintain the first creation.... Well-ordered states rose up where no single ray of revelation penetrated.... The light needed to form states is the light of nature." Etc.[91]

We here run up against multiple misconceptions, including an error regarding

6) special revelation

which we therefore treat together with 5).

... and special revelation

In the first place, it is not true that the government either in its origin or in its activity in history derives its light only from "common grace," is only in possession of "natural knowledge of God," or only participates in "general revelation." The origin of civil government lies in Genesis ch. 9, in which we are told of the institution of the Noahic covenant. What is the essence of the civil state? All power is from God (Romans 13: 1) and was first exercised by God alone, until, after the Flood, He transferred it to man, made in God's image.

---

[91] *The Herald,* nos. 1142, 1146, 1147, 1154 and 1156.

Dr. Kuyper's remark that this mandate "only served to maintain what exists and is in agreement with the natural impulse of man" betrays the unscriptural nature of his conception of common grace. We have to do here with a special revelation in the sphere of the redeemed, not only to maintain what exists, but also to prepare the way of redemption. It is bestowed after God's servant Noah offered the sacrifice of thanksgiving, bestowed upon them who received the promise of salvation before the expectation of salvation was restricted to the line of Shem. By means of that special revelation, we obtain more detailed knowledge about God's righteousness, but likewise of His mercy, longsuffering, and grace. What God has joined together, let no man tear asunder! It alarms us to no end to see the two sides split up and allocated among two exclusive spheres in accordance with a notional distinction, and within these two spheres, to two institutes, which certainly were not separated in the household of Noah.

But what we see at the origin of the administration of justice among men, can be spied in the entirety of history. Dr. Kuyper appears to be familiar with "well-ordered states ... where no single ray of revelation penetrated." Does he have a means properly to determine the extent of the influence exercised by Israel? Can he say with precision where the memories of Paradise were preserved and where they were not? Did Israel's prophets not "proclaim God's praise among the peoples;" did they, knowing "the fear of the Lord," not move people to faith and conversion? Will Dr. Kuyper assure us that the Spirit of the Lord did not operate to save souls outside of what he calls the sphere of particular grace?

We will soon hear him complain of the mixture, i.e., the insufficient distinction between church and state in the Old Covenant. Wrongly. But assuming [for the sake of argument] that he is correct about this, we would then also have to admit that no salvific knowledge of God was extended in Israel – the old point of contention between the Voetians and the Coccejans. For if, as a matter of principle, the sphere of particular grace is distinguished so much from that of common grace, and if the church first arose on Pentecost, this is the conclusion that would have to follow.

In the second place, Dr. Kuyper makes no distinction between the natural knowledge of God and the science of nature from which this knowledge of God is drawn. We hear him say, e.g., "The revelation of God is absolutely not restricted to the Word. Our Confession expressly states that we know God by two means: nature and Scripture. To this, therefore, pertains the knowledge of the entirety of created nature, the knowledge of science discovered through nature, the knowledge of the history of how God has guided the nations, and the knowledge of our own heart (!)."

And again:

"If someone asks, what must I do to be saved? No one can turn on the required light unless he takes that light from Holy Scripture." If on the other hand someone asks how the government is to rule.... "For the path of salvation, nature teaches nothing that leads you to that goal, only Holy Scripture does. But for the governing of states, nature teaches you a great deal, and the light of the Word only acts in a very auxiliary manner along with the light of nature.... a minister of the Word can only exercise his office and vocation by the light of Holy Scripture, but things are quite different for a doctor, a judge, a chemistry teacher, and quite different again for a gardener, a boatman."

We have already noted how this conception infringes upon the sufficiency of Holy Scripture. When one makes a proper distinction between science and the knowledge of God, which Dr. Kuyper does not do, then Holy Scripture is given not only to show us the way to salvation but also as the light by which everyone, always, in all circumstances, is to act. What he reckons to the sphere of particular grace, and what derives from general revelation and is a fruit of the natural knowledge of God, is found *in* Scripture just as well as *outside* it.

But just as dubious as the misconception of this character of Holy Scripture is the confusion between the knowledge of God and science. Our Confession indeed states that we know God through two means: nature and Scripture, but it also says that He has made Himself known more clearly and sufficiently in His Word. Dr. Kuyper forgot to emphasize the exordium, "He, God, makes *Himself* known to us." It therefore does *not* hold true for the world, for nature, for secondary causes. There is an innate natural knowledge of God that is multiplied and expanded by the contemplation of nature. But that is no reason to include in the knowledge of God the knowledge of categorizing plants into genera and families.

Obviously, the tanner needs to know all manner of things that Scripture cannot teach him, but that does not mean that what he knows of hides, tree bark and lye is to be called the Word of God!

In the third place, Dr. Kuyper's conception is so treacherous because science detached from Scripture, with an appeal to the insufficiency thereof, now, in the name of the natural knowledge of God, exerts its influence on theology.

Dr. Kuyper completely equates the Word of God in nature and in Scripture. And on the other hand, by virtue of this same theory, the church with its dogmatics exerts its influence on those whom Dr. Kuyper considers unauthorized to distinguish between existing confessions, i.e., between appearance and essence, content and form, truth and falsehood. "Nevertheless, this," namely the last quotation, regarding the natural knowledge of God, "does not rule out the church making the most of the light of common grace and the civil government taking advantage of the light of special revelation."[92] Thus far Dr. Kuyper.

This is fatal. If the theory was, here are two spheres that do not touch each other and never will, because they have their own origin, life, and purpose, then one could console himself with the thought that they each need to leave the other entirely alone. We have no tyranny to fear from either side. But now it seems that the state – which, by the way, will be expressly treated shortly – is quite amenable to the influence of a church regarding which it is not to judge in any shape, manner, or form. The truth that lies outside the state's horizon and does not pertain to the state's competence, indirectly brings the state under its dominion. And vice versa, there is the great danger that science, which has freed itself from the bond of the Confession, will begin to rule in the house of God.

In the fourth place, we here come across a proposition about the goal of special revelation, for which we do not gladly take responsibility. If our Confession states that God lets Himself be known even more clearly in His holy Word, it does not attribute an independent value to the natural knowledge of God, but hereby expresses that the knowledge of God that nature provides, only comes into its own when one has learned to know God in Holy Scripture. This

---

[92] *The Herald,* no. 1142.

knowledge must then be supplemented in the manner in which actuality supplements shadow, as the New Covenant supplements the Old.

Redemption is restoration.

Christ not only redeemed us from the penalty of sin, so that we have to work out our sanctification and redemption, but He fulfilled all righteousness for us, so that the gospel is not limited to a part of Christ's work, in the Roman Catholic way, which then is reckoned to particular grace, but comprehends everything that was corrupted in and through the first man. In other words, the entire Christ is at stake here, such as He is given to the church by the Father, as Lord and Head over all.

We encounter the same question again and again in another form – the political theory recommended by *The Herald*. [And in this connection] We now have to indicate a new error that is inherent to the three previous ones, especially the sufficiency of Scripture, namely,

7) that the Holy Spirit teaches us little or nothing about the relation between church and state.

Does the Bible have anything to say about Church and State?

Dr. Kuyper asks flatly in *The Herald:*[93] "Can we say that determinations and rules were established for the reciprocal relation of church and state, either by Jesus or by His apostles in His name, and can anyone show the places in which these determinations and rules are to be found in the New Testament?" But then he spares us the difficulty. "It may safely be said that not one single reference exists that reveals to a well-disposed magistrate: with regard to the church you must conduct yourself in such and such a manner."

He goes even further and takes it upon himself to search for an explanation for the fact that many brothers invoked the Old Testament "to their hurt." The reason for this, he says, is "the complete absence of anything relevant to this matter in the New Testament."

---

[93] *The Herald,* no. 1147.

"The silence of the New Testament has tempted many brothers to seek in the Old Testament to supplement what was lacking the New Testament, to their hurt."

As it turns out, they did not find much respite in the Old Testament either, for the following reason: "What existed in Israel either before or after the exile can establish no law or rule here, and cannot even serve as an example. In a theocracy, the magistrate functions in an entirely different position than among the nations, and therefore in Israel as well the church lacked every instituted, independent organization separate from national life."

We miss in the above reference any indication at all that Prof. Kuyper has become acquainted with the scriptural grounds which "many brothers" in the 16th and 17th centuries invoked against the Anabaptist, Libertine, Lutheran, Puritan, Romish, and Remonstrant concepts in the area of state law and the law of nations. If it is an error to think that the Old Testament sheds any light for us regarding life in the state, then "brother" Trigland and "brother" Voetius were seriously guilty of that error.

We thus give a flat answer to the flat question asked in the first of the above citations, namely, not to the question as here posed but to the question that *should* have been posed. "Rules for the relation between the modern state and the church brought into agreement with that state" are certainly not to be found. Whether the church is placed in the framework of a private association or is recognized in public law as an ecclesiastical fiscal entity, makes no difference in this regard.[94] But if, and this must be the case if Isaiah 66: 3 is applicable to us, if we investigate Scripture without preconceived notions – not to confirm our previous conception, not to silence those who disagree with us, but to know the will of the Lord in this matter and thus to consult the divine oracle – then in both the Old and the New Testaments we will find everything we need rightly to understand the question under consideration, and much more than we might expect.

---

[94] See above, pp. 42ff.

Yes, the Bible has something to say about Church and State

We discover a clear indication of the origin of authority, the evidence that the government is God's steward and that its authority descends from above rather than ascends from below, more specifically descends from God as Creator and not Christ as Mediator; that the government therefore does not owe its origin and existence to the church; that it is God's pleasure to rule us by its hand; that we are called to obedience not out of fear but for conscience' sake; that this obedience has its limit in duties to God; that ruler and subject, citizen and citizens, parents and children, and so forth, stand in such and such mutual relation; that the government possesses a coercive power; that no specific form of government is prescribed; that the church is the revelation of the body of Christ in the world; therefore, it does not owe its origin and existence to the civil government and cannot be made dependent upon the government's pleasure in any way, shape, or form; that that church has no visible Head, nor can it; that it must be able to do everything necessary to the building up of the body of Christ; that the civil government only possesses an external ordering [ordineerende] power over the church; that the public interpretation of the Word is entrusted to the church; that the nations are brought to Christ as nations; that legislation and public policy must be in agreement with the law of nature and morality, and with that which God has revealed in His Word in this matter; that the neutrality of the civil government is a nullity; that the civil government ought to accept the truth which the church confesses and the light which it kindles for the proper understanding of the Word, to the degree necessary to fulfill its vocation; that God is the Lord of conscience; that faith cannot and ought not be evoked by force; that no external advantages are to be attached to the profession of the name of the Lord; that the government may not be made dependent upon the vicissitudes of public opinion; that the church and the truth should not seek their strength through calculations in terms of a numerical majority or a coalition.

Is it really so difficult to demonstrate and elucidate these and a hundred other theses in which an answer is given to the questions which come up in the discussion surrounding Article 36 of our Confession? We gladly take up the challenge to provide that evidence from Scripture. But before doing so, we must demonstrate that the question to which we just gave an affirmative answer, proceeds from an incorrect premise.

8) Dr. Kuyper errs in his concept of the church.

Kuyper's Erroneous Views on the Church

The state, the subject of the *Herald* series of articles we are now discussing, is the state such as we know it as children of the 19th century, the state as what it became under the influence of the [French] Revolution. And the church of which the writer speaks is not the church as it must be or become in terms of God's idea, but everything "that identifies as Church." This seems to be quite practical and very generous, but apart from the fact that this manner of posing the question hopelessly confuses the issue, and regardless of the fact that the well-known statement made at the Middelburg assembly is hereby made a mockery,[95] and besides all manner of other objections, such as the already-mentioned complaint that this kind of treatment infringes on the authority of Holy Scripture – beyond this, it is so fatal because Dr. Kuyper, if he had stuck to the Word, would immediately have discovered the error in his concept of the church.

We will now demonstrate this.

He speaks continually of the instituted church and hereby equates the temporal form and the immutable essence. This is likewise the major error of the Nonconformity and the demonstration of the truth of what we have continuously stated in all manner of polemical writings, that the deviation from the Confession of the Reformed church in the area of political theory led to the schism in the church. The fundamentally Romish dualism between church and state, expressed in, e.g., the above-mentioned doctrines of the two spheres and of common grace, make Dr. Kuyper's politics too broad and his theology too narrow. But the consequence of this generosity *in politicis* is again felt in theology. We are hereby kept from seeing how it is that the unity of the church is sacrificed by putting the institutional element of the church in the foreground.

---

[95] If one wishes to show that our fathers were wrong, one should first establish what it is they actually taught.

In this respect, the Nonconformity in its belligerent origins was consistent to some extent. [In its view,] The national Reformed church was no church anymore, and the offices in that church were unfilled. But the logical conclusion of this theory, that knows the visible church only as institute,[96] extends much farther. Any who deviate with regard to the institute are in fact no church at all, when judged by this standard. Rome alone draws the conclusion, but in principle it inheres in Dr. Kuyper's conception.

He understands "by Church as institute, a circle of persons who live in church relation, and express this relation in confession and church order."[97] Many things can be deduced from this conception. In the first place, it is clear as day that his entire opposition to Article 36, to the degree that it touches upon a principle, stems from this misconception regarding the actual question, and more specifically from his church concept, which deviates from our Confession.

Dr. Kuyper sees all manner of churches or denominations differing in a myriad of ways from each other, and asks not, how are we to judge among those churches according to God's Word and our Confession, but rather, how can the civil government, which has other things to do, render a judgement regarding these splintered questions that are attached to this pluriformity, of which there are so many that have nothing to do with spiritual life? Were it conceivable that the churches could lay aside their mutual differences to act as a unity vis-à-vis civil government, then the objection that now exists in his mind would entirely fall to the ground.

Apropos, we read the following in *The Herald*, no. 1186:

---

[96] [This seems to contradict the understanding of church-as-organism as likewise an expression of the visible church, as put forward in Kuyper's *Encyclopedia of Sacred Theology* (Dutch edition), vol. 3. But note this statement in *The Herald*, no. 1187: "Spiritually the souls of the faithful were set free of the domination of the ecclesiastical powerholders, thereby indicating the distinction between the visible church institute and the invisible inside of the church as the organic body of Christ" (*Common Grace* (Dutch ed.), vol. 3, p. 246; see also p. 43 above).]

[97] *The Herald,* no. 1155.

"As long as the church acts in one shape or form with one confession, as an inward and outward whole, then we have no difference of opinion whatsoever about the task that the civil government has to fulfill with regard to this one church." This shows (for the umpteenth time) that Dr. Kuyper has no fundamental and thus insoluble objection to Article 36 arising from the distinction between the above-mentioned two spheres. At the least, this yields a significant concession.

In the second place, his definition of the church as institute gives rise to an amusing and not unimportant misconception. He, namely, demands flatly that we answer the following question: "How is the civil government, if it encounters on its terrain more than one visible church, to decide which is the true one? ... If is it to protect the *true* church and remove all idolatry and false religion, then should it not begin by deciding what here is the true form of the church?"[98]

"As long as they do not flatly and conclusively answer this objection," he says, "they have no right to speak to the issue of the relation between church and state."

In the same connection, however, we are assured that our fathers' political viewpoints were determined by their notion that only one church was possible. According to Kuyper, our fathers accepted: "1. that only one form of Christ's church was possible for God, and that all other formations identifying themselves as such were false imitations; 2. that the government has just as much to choose the church in its only true formation, as it is obligated to repulse and oppose the imitation."

Our fathers, the Reformers, indeed assumed the *unity* of the church. On this basis, they said that they left "the court of Rome," not the Catholic church. But for that reason the one church was *not* the instituted church, the church bound to a specific church government. For the marks of the true church are indicated in Article 29. After treating of the offices and ministers of the church in separate articles, Article 32 treats of "The Order and Discipline of the Church." It was considered "useful and beneficial, that those, who are rulers of the Church, institute and establish certain ordinances among themselves" for certain goals;

---

[98] *The Herald,* no. 1187.

but independent of this order, *the church* already existed, and already was everything that is said about this church.

Even apart from this, Dr. Kuyper's viewpoint is invalid. For in the days of Calvin and Guido de Bres, the church was not as uniform as he would have us believe. From their conception of the church of the Old and the New Covenants, it followed of necessity that for them church unity did not depend upon a church form.

In the third place, we all of a sudden discover what in his view constituted the novelty and peculiarity of Calvinism. It is not said in so many words, for then it could be contradicted, but it is now included in the argument, apart from any evidence – it is *freedom of conscience* (!).

We read as follows in the Stone Lectures:[99]

I do not build therefore on subterfuge, but I appeal to clear historical facts. And here I repeat the underlying characteristic of Calvinism must be sought, not in what it has adopted from the past, but in what it has newly created. It is remarkable, in this connection, that, from the very beginning, our Calvinistic Theologians and jurists have defended liberty of conscience against the Inquisition. Rome perceived very clearly how liberty of conscience must loosen the foundations of the unity of the visible Church, and therefore she opposed it. But on the other hand it must be admitted that Calvinism, by praising aloud liberty of conscience, has in principle abandoned every absolute characteristic of the visible Church.

As soon as in the bosom of one and the same people the conscience of one half witnessed against that of the other half, the breach had been accomplished, and placards were no longer of any avail. As early as 1649 it was declared that persecution, for faith's sake, was—'A spiritual murder, an assassination of the soul, a rage against God himself, the most horrible of sins.' And it is evident that Calvin himself wrote down the premises of the correct conclusion, by his acknowledgment that against atheists even the Catholics are our allies.[100]

---

[99] *Lectures on Calvinism*, p. 102.

[100] [Here the Dutch translation of the lectures, which Hoedemaker cites, has "… by his acknowledgement of Roman Catholic baptism."]

What he says here is partly incorrect, partly irrelevant, but as stated leads to conclusions entirely different from those he draws, indeed, completely opposite ones. But these are secondary matters.

His view of the church as institute

It is time to examine more closely the writer's starting point, the instituted church. Rome not only assumes that the church first manifests itself as an external organization, i.e., as institute, but also that it is organized into a specific, prescribed form. For this reason, Bellarmine taught that the notion of a church that is invisible, or that is visible (in the offices) but has no prescribed form, is not only incorrect but also absurd.[101] Moehler wrote, "The Catholics teach: the visible Church is first, then comes the invisible; the former gives birth to the latter. On the other hand, the Lutherans say the reverse: from the invisible emerges the visible Church.... In this apparently very unimportant opposition, a prodigious difference is avowed."[102]

Moehler's way of thinking is Dr. Kuyper's as well. The church is not the revelation of the body of Christ, but something else.

> The conception of the instituted Church is much narrower than the Church of Christ when taken as the body of Christ, for this includes in itself all the powers and workings that arise from re-creation. There is a Christian disposition and a Christian fellowship, there is a Christian knowledge and a Christian art, etc., which indeed spring from the field of the Church and can flourish on this field alone, but which by no means therefore proceed from the instituted Church. The instituted Church finds her province bounded by her offices.[103]

We find with him, then, the same relation between the visible and the invisible church as with the Roman Catholics. Regarding Romans 10: 14, "How shall they hear without a preacher?" he notes, "The visible church lies in these

---

[101] Bellarmine, *De Eccl. Mil.* [Of the Church Militant], 1, 12, 13, 15, in *Opera Omnia,* tomus secundus.

[102] Moehler, *Symbolism,* p. 398.

[103] Kuyper, *Encyclopedia of Sacred Theology,* pp. 587–588.

words.... It is now the case that the church or the army [keurbende] of Christ needs an institute in which the ministry of the Word can take place, in order to be gathered, in order to be armed and trained, and in order to be reproduced from generation to generation."

"This is all that the visible church is: it is simply an institute for the ministry of the Word, an institute established by the church and for the church.... The institute of the visible church finds its origin and cause only in the ministry of the Word"(!).[104]

In a discussion about the church, we must first and foremost take into consideration that this word can be used in more than one way. If we neglect to pay attention to this, we continually run the risk of drawing wrong conclusions, because the concept "church" has not been kept pure. Dr. Kuyper's articles on church and state offer us many examples. For example, Question 54 of the Heidelberg Catechism teaches "that the Son of God from the beginning to the end of the world, gathers, defends, and preserves to himself by his Spirit and word, out of the whole human race, a church chosen to everlasting life, agreeing in true faith."[105] If we ask Dr. Kuyper how this accords with the conception in *The Herald* "that civil government was there [er was] as soon as the patriarchal authority collapsed, but the church did not arise as an independent entity until Pentecost"[106] and in the *Encyclopedia of Sacred Theology,* where it speaks of "the institutes of the ecumenical church as these were founded by Christ and His apostles,"[107] he answers that Question 54 "rules out any identification of the church with the institute. One only remains in the institute temporarily, while he remains in the organism eternally."[108]

---

[104] *E Voto Dordaceno* [I agree with Dort], vol. II, p. 134.

[105] *The Three Forms of Unity,* p. 7.

[106] *The Herald,* no. 1155.

[107] *Encyclopedia of Sacred Theology* (Dutch edition), vol. 3 (Kampen: J. H. Kok, 1909²), p. 226.

[108] *Ibid.,* p. 216. [This again points to the inconsistency in Kuyper's doctrine of the visible church, for in this instance the church-as-organism is equated with the eternal, thus invisible, church. See also n. 96.]

Another example. The most important marks of the true church, according to our Confession, are the pure preaching of the gospel and the administration of the sacraments in agreement therewith. It follows from this that there may be all manner of things wrong with a church, but we may not separate from it if these two are found there. Point this out to Dr. Kuyper and ask him how things in the church life of those calling themselves Reformed [i.e., the Nonconformists] can be reconciled with this, he informs us that "the ministry of the Word with all that accompanies it, does not pertain to the body of Christ in its actual *essence.*"

We could continue like this, but for our purposes these two examples are sufficient. With regard to the first example: The remark that one does not remain a member of the Reformed church for eternity is almost too naïve. What was the question again? Kuyper said that the church had no independent existence under the Old Testament. The Catechism disagreed, and spoke of the one church in both the Old and New Testaments, showing that this unity must refer to the visible, but *not* the institutional church. What does Dr. Kuyper now do? Misled by the ambiguity of the word, he makes his opinion, which deviates from the Confession, into a measure of the Confession, allowing him to neglect to draw the conclusion: my church concept differs from the Heidelberg Catechism's.

The second example is even more crass. The Confession here speaks of the visible church. This was difficult to deny, but all of a sudden, the entire visible church stands outside the church "in its actual essence." Nonetheless, the contrary holds; we recall that the visible and invisible church are not two churches but two sides of the same phenomenon. Whatever during the course of the ages has changed in the outward manifestation of the church – the offices, the gifts of grace, the forms of communal exercise – the Head, the life, the covenant, and the seals of the covenant have remained unchanged.

The Roman Catholics indeed posed the following dilemma to the Protestants: "You claim that certain errors in the church make it into a false church. Now then, these so-called errors are not from today or yesterday but from of old. One or the other is true: either they long ago rendered the church exanimate, or the church lives until this day despite those errors. But in either case you leave the church."

Our fathers gave this answer: far be it from us! We only depart from the soul-destroying errors. We only separate ourselves from the creature-worship. We recognize in you what is of the Word, as the revelation of the true church. We never separated ourselves from the baptism, the eucharist, the first three Catholic creeds.

This already shows how incorrect the claim is that the civil government only comes into contact with the church as institute – the cardinal point in the Dr. Kuyper's exposition in *The Herald.*

Yet other errors either derive from or are connected with Dr. Kuyper's conception, the discussion of which must of necessity come first. The opinion, for example, that

9) The church under the Old Testament had no independent existence.

The church in the Old Testament

According to Dr. Kuyper, in Israel there was an office with a spiritual character, but we cannot say that the church in Israel "was separately instituted." One did not belong to the church in Israel by "confession, but by descent from the Jewish people." The Sanhedrin was "vested" with political and ecclesiastical "power." "We find the church in a more independent capacity in the synagogues, but the ecclesiastical office did not exist there.... Under these conditions it is somewhat surprising that earlier generations, including our fathers, were of the opinion that they could derive so much from the Old Testament to support their positions."

Dr. Kuyper supposes that they did this not because of partiality[109] but because the New Testament did not give them any data for their system (!). We already dismissed the latter proposition. Furthermore, we explained the entire conception that, as we said, infringes the authority, the perspicuity, and the sufficiency of Holy Scripture by referencing a concept of church and state that deviates from Scripture. If, instead of asking, child-like, what Scripture says, we come to Scripture with a proposition derived from empirical reality or corresponding to human notions and desires, then it does not reveal its treasures, but is a partially closed, partially (or entirely) misunderstood book, even for the most learned investigator.

---

[109] *The Herald,* no. 1154.

Dr. Kuyper's claim that "one did not belong to the church in Israel by profession but by descent from the Jewish people" could elicit from us the question: you are a teacher in Israel and you do not know these things? Unless he is prepared to defend the Anabaptist position that the Old Covenant was a national covenant, to abandon infant baptism, and to deny that Abraham and his seed partake of the same salvation that is bestowed on us in Christ, as well as circumcision being a "seal of justification by faith,"[110] then he can find no reasonable ground for this opinion, which likewise deviates from the viewpoint of the Reformed church.

Scripture clearly teaches that grace is not inherited. This notion is as it were a pattern in accordance with which the entire history of salvation is effectuated. It is illustrated in a variety of ways in the Old Testament as well.

While circumcision was obligatory for all of Abraham's descendants and for those born in his house, there were times during the history of Israel that the covenant was suspended and circumcision was not carried out. During the 38-year ban, the people was not circumcised. Only upon the entry into Canaan at Gilgal was Israel's reproach removed. Consider the lepers who were cut off from church communion without ceasing to be members of the people. Above all, attend to the relation between Israel and foreigners.

We expressly treated this subject in the first volume of *Sword and Trowel,*[111] from which we borrow the following:

The foreigner (*gér*) living in the land belonged to the people, as distinguished from the traveler (*nokhri*), Deut. 29: 10; Deut. 14: 21; 15: 3; 33: 20; Lev. 24: 10; the sojourner (*toshab*); the Nethinim, the slaves, the proselytes, as well as the sons of Israel.

Foreigners enjoyed many privileges in Israel. They fell under the Lord's special protection, Deut. 10: 18; Ps. 146: 9.

Their rights were maintained, Ex. 22; 21; 23: 9; Deut. 24: 7. By all manner of statutes the expression follows: "You will have one law both for the foreigner and the native" Ex. 12: 49; Lev. 24: 22.

---

[110] Romans 4: 11.

[111] [See n. 5 1.]

General religious obligations and rights were in force for foreigners. They had to guard themselves from certain abominations, Lev. 17: 10.

They could bring sacrifices, 1 Kings 8: 38; participate in the feasts, Deut. 16: 11. Sacrifices for sin redounded to their benefit, Lev. : 8 [presumably 22: 18]; Num. 15: 14.

The foreigner was not obligated to be circumcised. John Hyrcanus acted contrary to law when he forced the Edomites to be circumcised, as did Aristobulus with regard to the Iturians.

One could become a member of the church without gaining the right of citizenship, and one could be a citizen, in full possession of all rights, and at the same time be cut off from church communion. The former applied to the gate proselytes and the righteous proselytes, while the latter applied to the unclean, the leprous, and the censured.

Ezechiel opened to foreigners the prospect of the right of landownership, Ez. 47: 22.

Many foreigners (the number of whom was very large, Num. 11: 4; 2 Chr. 2: 17) occupied leading positions. For instance, Uriah the Hittite, and Arauna, who was not a proselyte ("The Lord your God," 2 Sam. 24: 24).

The path to church communion was open to all peoples, with some reservation regarding certain peoples, and with the exclusion of the Canaanites. Abraham was required to circumcise everyone in his house.

Circumcision gave the right to participate in the covenant meal, the Passover (Ex. 12: 44), while the slaves of priests might even eat of the holy food. In this way one entered "the assembly of the Lord," Deut. 23: 8.

Such foreigners who came to Judaism were called proselytes (Greek *proselytus*) in later centuries and were distinguished between righteous proselytes and gate proselytes (cf. Ex. 20: 10; Deut. 14: 21).

This indicates the distinction between citizens and members, and therefore also between church and people.

That one could be a member of the one church in Israel even though one did not live under the same government, was demonstrated during the period of the Judges, when the tribes were fairly loosely connected. But especially when Israel was split into two kingdoms. Jeroboam hindered the people from going to Jerusalem, but in terms of the essence of the matter, the split that pitted

Judah and Ephraim against each other did not form a hindrance to this. It became a schism in the church because of political considerations, against which the anonymous prophet from Judah at Bethel, and the invitation from Hezekiah and Josiah for a joint celebration of Passover, protested strongly.

The people, and thus the church, were under foreign rule in Egypt, in Assyria, in Babylon, and in Israel itself (under Gedaliah).

The idea of "church," i.e., the more specific and closer union of believers under one head, does not contradict this. Therefore, the entire polemic against the national church does not have the least foundation.

It therefore appears that "church and state in Israel" were truly distinguished to the degree that the citizen was not necessarily a member of the church. The same can be said of the offices, the officers, and official power. The priests had no constitutional rank, and assisted the judge only as expounders of the law (Deut. 17: 8–12, 21: 10). The tribal princes constantly come to the fore (Num. 36: 1; Deut. 29: 9, 10; 1 Chr. 27: 16).

Things changed after the Exile. The priests occupied themselves more and more with affairs of state and the high priest *de facto* competed for the kingship. All of this, however, lies outside the terrain of revelation and deviated from the custom, while also being in conflict with the law. Dr. Kuyper could have derived the argument in service of the position he defends just as well from the composition of the States General.

The disobedient son was brought to the elders in his city (Deut. 21: 19; cf. 22: 15; 25: 7; 29: 12). The elders may have been joined together with the priests into a judicial college by Jehoshaphat, but "the affairs of the Lord" were always distinguished from the affairs of the king.

Prior to the days of the New Covenant, the church was not instituted in the sense that it acted as a separate institution with a local manifestation, a prescribed order, and extended assemblies of officers, but that does not mean it was invisible. After all, the close relation between church and state that we note in Israel was a direct consequence not of some lack in its religious life in the Old Covenant, of the Old Testament dispensation, but of the relation to which God stood with this people. The distinction between ceremonial, judicial, and moral laws draws attention to this. But it appears from the offices, the covenant seals, the religious gatherings and the exercise of discipline that the church was also public in Israel, and the first duty of the civil government was to assist it in its prophetic vocation.

On the other hand, Dr. Kuyper could never have stated that the civil government only comes into contact with the church as institute, if he did not harbor an error precisely regarding the church's prophetic vocation

10) to profess the truth.

The prophetic vocation of the church in the public square

Dr. Kuyper argues that Article 36 does not belong in the Confession. It was included when no one thought it conceivable that there would be more than one church and the difference of opinion only concerned the question, is the church here, or is it under the Pope? "In its Confession the church gives account of itself *to the civil magistrate*." But this government does not have the right to judge in the theological controversy regarding church law and liturgy and to give preference to one orientation over another.[112]

In the opinion of Dr. Kuyper, this restricts the character and subject matter of the Confession. In our view it would follow from the above assumption, when seen in the context of Dr. Kuyper's viewpoint, that at present the Confession can be entirely given up, since the government no longer looks to it, and it has ceased to be the ground on which freedom of religion is granted.

Might one not also take from this that there should never have been a confession? After all, if the civil government, to use Dr. Kuyper's terminology, stands on the terrain of "common grace," and as such must be considered unauthorized to judge regarding that which pertains to "particular grace," then it would not have asked for such an account. If it had not asked for it, then the church should not have tendered it, etc.

But the assumption is wrong. In his introduction to Rotterdam's commentary on the Belgic Confession,[113] Dr. Kuyper correctly stated, following Maresius, that a confession serves "1) to distinguish pure churches from those outside; 2) to defend the truth against error; 3) to preserve the unity of the church; 4) to indicate the boundaries within which the minister of the Word can freely move in his proclamation of the truth." Such things can be read

---

[112] *The Herald,* nos. 1186 and 1187.

[113] *Zions Roem en Sterkte* [Zion's Fame and Strength] (Rotterdam: Gebr. Huge, 1860).

among all the Reformed divines. À Marck adds "that the members and teachers of the church are so tightly bound to the confession by their solemn assurance, that they cannot reject it and remain a member of the community in question."[114] The Confession therefore is not only necessary for the magistrate, but also for the church itself, for its members and teachers. It should contain not only that which is necessary to know to be saved, but everything that corresponds with the revelation, in particular, the vocation of the church and the rights as well as the duties of officers.

The boundary between the ecclesiastical and the civil power belongs here in the first place, certainly not the last. Peter Martyr wrote as follows:

> In this manner, then, the ecclesiastical power comprehends all matters, because it finds its counsel regarding all matters in God's Word. For there is nothing in the entire world to which the Word of God does not extend. For this reason they err greatly who are wont to call out: what does the preacher have to do with the Republic, and with weapons, and with cooks! Rather let them say, should ministers find the Word of God being transgressed in such matters, why should they not punish it and admonish from the Word of God that they should give up sin. They are competent to punish, not with the sword, not with prison, not with exile, but with the power of the divine Word.[115]

This may be said particularly of preaching, but it presupposes the right and duty of the church to act in its confession as "teacher sent from God," conditional upon the appeal to God's Word and the right [of each] to render an individual, independent judgement regarding the truth.

---

[114] *Het merch der christelijke godtsgeleertheit* [The Marrow of Christian Divinity] (Amsterdam: Borstius, 1705), ch. XXXIII, sec. XX.

[115] Peter Martyr Vermigli, *Loci communes* [Fundamental doctrinal themes], classis quartae, caput XIII, sec. 9.

Should any doubt exist on this point, one should consult the *Acta* regarding the struggle against the teachings of the Remonstrants.[116] It is therefore an error to think that God has revealed something in His Word that faith does not have to accept, or that the mouth does not need to express what the heart believes.

But this error is rooted in the disregard of the vocation of the church regarding

11) The public interpretation of the Word.

Public versus Magisterial Vocation of the Church

We are not entirely sure whether this is an error to which Dr. Kuyper has been brought by his deviation from our church's political principle. But we are faced here with a curious case.

One should assume that a scholar like Dr. Kuyper, so well-schooled in Reformed theology, is aware of the distinction between the *authoritative* interpretation of Holy Scripture, which the Roman church arrogates to itself, and the *public* interpretation of Scripture which is entrusted to the church. He should know that the full authority which is due to the truth discovered by the light of revelation is to be attributed to this public interpretation, but only with the implicit assumption of the right of private interpretation, and its conformity with God's Word. Yet in everything he has written regarding these matters, there is nothing that betrays even the slightest hint of this indispensable and fully adequate distinction.

To the question, in what way does the civil government come to know the principles by which it is to govern? Dr. Kuyper answers, "three answers are conceivable.

"In the first place, one can say that it is the role of the church to indicate this, and as we know, Rome supplied this answer."

Quite so.

---

[116] "De algemeene consideratiën door de Remonstranten ingeleverd ter Dordsche Synode" [The general considerations submitted by the Remonstrants at the Synod of Dort]. Voetius, *Politica Ecclesiastica* [Ecclesiastical Politics] Partis Primae Libri III. Tract. I cap. IV, V.

But the Reformed church also gave an answer to this question, yet one which is *entirely different!* Teacher in Israel, do you not know these things?

The opposite is apparent from his quite modest demand, to which everyone gladly will subscribe. "We do not desire that any Reformed church be given the right to decide on the divine ordinances in the political field in accordance with the Word, on behalf of the civil government in a country like ours."[117] The only difficulty with this axiomatic position is that the writer appears to suggest that such a demand might even be asserted from the Reformed side.

In another place, though, Dr. Kuyper again reasons as if it were the Reformed view that the government has to draw knowledge of all manner of things lying outside its sphere directly from Holy Scripture, without regard to the church and the ministry of the Word.

Wrongly.

Our Reformed divines took a different view of the matter. Trigland wrote:

> All the Reformed have unanimously and steadfastly attributed this (distinguishing) judgement to the faithful, and on this basis opposed the implicit faith (*fides implicita*) of the Roman church.
>
> But this does not cancel the judgement of the pastors and teachers of the church, but instead confirms and establishes it. For if it is the right of all believers to judge the doctrine transmitted to them, then this right must be attributed even more to those to whom Christ Himself has entrusted the care of the church and the power to teach in it, Eph. 4: 12–14.[118]

Musculus wrote:

> Those who administer the teaching office in the church are officially obligated to teach not only subjects but also magistrates regarding how they are to behave and to punish the sinful.

---

[117] *The Standard,* 16 May 1878.

[118] Jacobus Trigland, *Antapologia: sive examen refutatio totius apologiae Remonstrantium* [Antapology: or a refuting examination of all the Remonstrants' apologies] (Amsterdam: Joannem Janssonium, 1664), p. 46.

If kings, princes, and other magistrates have subjected themselves to the yoke of Christ, the ministers of the Word by virtue of their office are not only allowed but commanded to implant in them the faithfulness, care and diligence by which they ought to serve Christ the Lord, king of kings; according to the words of David, 'And now, you kings, allow yourselves to be taught, you judges on earth, serve the Lord with fear.'[119]

Furthermore, W. Teelinck,[120] G. Udemans,[121] and others. Voetius wrote:

When the church brings the Word of the heavenly King to the magistrate, it does this as a messenger. In the meantime, the magistrate remains magistrate whether he gives heed to this Word or not, and retains his rulership even if he abuses his power.

A husbandman or young man who has been accepted as a guide, is, insofar as he shows the way to the captain of the whole army, the commander's guide.

In this way he is also first in leading, but by way of ministering, not as the superior himself, nor as the equal of the general.[122]

We may not separate the political principle of our Confession from Articles 27–34, as well as the doctrine of church offices, more specifically from the ministry of the Word and in connection with this, the public interpretation of that

---

[119] W. Musculus, "De Magistratibus [Of the Magistrate]," in *Loci Communes sacrae Theologiae* [Fundamental Themes in Sacred Theology], quoted in Trigland, "Van d'authoriteyt der hoogher Overheydt [Regarding the Authority of the High Magistracy]," in *Christelycke ende nootwendighe verclaringhe* etc. [Christian and necessary statement], pp. 61–62.

[120] W. Teelinck, *Den politycken christen: ofte Instructie voor alle hooge en lage overheidspersonen* [The political Christian: instruction for all greater and lesser magistrates] (Middelburg: Anthony de Later, 1650).

[121] G. Udemans, *'t Geestelyck roer van 't coopmans schip* [The spiritual rudder of the merchant ship] (Dordrecht: François Boels, 1655), Book 6, ch. 3, pp. 517ff.

[122] [No attribution given.]

Word in Articles 30 and 31. If we do this, we run the grave risk of falling into the snare that Dr. Kuyper could not avoid. After all, if the civil government is not competent or capable of establishing according to Scripture the truth that it recognizes, which it wishes to lay as the foundation of its governing policy, this means one of three things: either it rules entirely according to its own will – *autocracy* – or it decides for itself what is good and evil, truth and falsehood – *absolutism* – or that it has no independent judgement but stands entirely under the influence either of the numerical majority or of public opinion – *the doctrine that we have to combat, especially in this connection*.

We therefore take up the cudgels for the Reformed as opposed to the Romish principle of interpretation, but in terms of this principle, for the freedom and independence of the civil government. Because by the standpoint we here combat, the government is like a gauge registering whatever opinion is dominant at a given point in time.

We now show how in this context the supposition of the incompetence of the civil government to choose between good and evil of necessity leads to

12) the slavish subjection of the civil government to the predominant opinion of the moment, which, as matters now stand, will eventually lead to Rome.

The Threat of Subjection to Rome

That the civil government is partly incompetent, partly incapable – *The Herald* is not consistent on this point – of acting according to the light of Scripture, is a position that is substantiated in this series of *Herald* articles, sometimes in this manner, sometimes in that.[123]

"One must be born again to see the kingdom of God," reasons Dr. Kuyper; "from this it follows that this sphere and everything pertaining to it, factually lies outside the horizon of the civil government and will always have to lie outside it, even when the magistrate is born again, because the office does not get born again."

"The universal Christian church," he elsewhere argues, "was split into a multiplicity of churches after the Reformation of the 16th century, so that sagacity

---

[123] *The Herald*, nos. 1175 ff.

and spiritual knowledge is necessary to distinguish the true from the false in this field."

If, because of the incapacity noted above, the civil government is completely incompetent both to see the kingdom of God (here equated with the church and the truth) and to be born again, then in our view it cannot see one church, let alone a hundred. We therefore cannot comprehend what difference the pluriformity of the church makes in this relation. The fields of the church and of the state are so far apart that one cannot even say that the civil government, which according to Dr. Kuyper's system does not interfere with the church, is "neutral." Simply because it has nothing to do with the church.

"The minister of water management," we hear Dr. Kuyper say, "is entirely indifferent to whether allopathic as opposed to homeopathic medicine is true, but is not for this reason neutral.... What does the engineer, who oversees dykes and sluices, have in common with the physician?" You see, it works out precisely.

We therefore are as little in agreement with his presupposition and argumentation as we are with his conclusion. But in this context we are only concerned with the question as to whether the division of the church into churches is the basis for which the civil government is denied the right to judge in cases concerning religion.[124]

It seems to us that Dr. Kuyper must be aware that his conception of "institute" is playing tricks on him. His argument reminds us of a plea conducted in a debating society of jurists in favor of someone accused of bad faith, as demonstrated by not returning a borrowed object. The defense proved 1) that his client had never received the object in question, 2) that it was completely useless when he received it, and 3) that it was returned on time and in good order!

The civil government should indeed be able to interfere with the church "and even go much farther than Rome desires" if only there was one church, but not now! Now that the principle of "freedom of conscience,"[125] we hear him say,

---

[124] With the understanding that this involves matters that concern it. This is the intention of our fathers, and not otherwise.

[125] Another arrow in Rome's quiver.

"has penetrated the Protestant church and the unity of believers has been splintered by increasing knowledge and development,"[126] so that "the civil government not only would have to choose between various churches and sects, but also between diverging orientations within the pale of the same church, it must be clear to everyone who thinks about this that it is virtually impossible to choose between all of these."[127] This argument is undergirded by the remark that "the vocation of the civil government cannot extend further than the gifts allotted to it, among which the spiritual light does not pertain" (!).

If the administration of justice took place outside of morality, if the government had nothing to do with religion, if no scientific principle at all underlay legislation, then it would speak for the conception that disputes the right of civil government to pass independent judgement over certain matters, the conception which makes civil government equal to the boy in the bowling alley who sets up the ministries that the ballot box knocks over. But now, unless we take the majority rather than the truth as our standard, there is no choice between the already rejected revolutionary theory of state law and the Reformed principle "that the state authority is bound neither directly nor through the pronouncement of any church, but only in the conscience of the ruling authority and to God's will."[128]

---

[126] *The Herald,* no. 1187.

[127] *The Herald,* nos. 1189, 1192.

[128] The expression "bound in the consciences" is derived, with one minor modification, from *Our Program* [H. here references Article 3, p. 1. The original version reads, "In the area of statecraft as well, the anti-revolutionary orientation confesses the eternal principles of God's Word, but in such a manner that the state authority is bound neither directly nor through the pronouncement of any church to the ordinances of God, but only in the conscience of government personnel."]

It does not suit the principle there recommended, but only the principle rejected in the Belgic Confession. If the civil government does not have the right to bind itself to a certain confession, the above-mentioned expression is empty words. As soon as the context of his argument leads to this, Dr. Kuyper knows how to make it very clear. In his

The Reformed did not ask for slavish subjection but only *reasonable* conviction. In this respect, they made no distinction between a Christian and a heathen, a believing and an unbelieving civil government. As a member of the church, the magistrate was subjected to the power of the church and as such stood on the same level with other members. But he was not obligated to membership.

In ch. 25 of the Apology against the Remonstrants[129] (p. 300) the distinction between the Romish and the Reformed conception is indicated in this manner:

1) According to the Roman Catholics, the government protects the church as its servant, while according to the Reformed it does so as ruler.

---

essay cited above, in which he seeks to provide evidence that it was of no practical use to insist on revision of Article 36 "since this article cannot be implemented anyway," we hear him say:

"Whether or not the government is 'a Christian government' does not depend on what you, as a citizen, think of it or say about it, and even less the question whether the people in government behave in a Christian way; something like that must emerge from an act of state, from an official document, as a charter of a decision lawfully taken. If our constitution were a Christian one, it should be made clear from the constitution, as it was demonstrated in the past by the accord of the seven provinces."

Absolutely true. Which is why we believe that it is popular deception to give the impression that the religious content of the people's representatives is able to neutralize the influence of a quasi-neutral constitutional system, and why we insist on constitutional revision in the Dutch sense. This principle that the civil magistrate is bound only in his conscience, which is only appropriate to the Reformed system, now remains without any significance .... that is, until a member of a church-oriented party acquires the power of government and, considering himself bound only in conscience, easily exceeds his competence.

[129] [Source unknown.]

2) According to Rome, the church judges with an infallible judgement, which
the government, like everyone else, must accept without further investigation.
3) According to the Reformed, the government retains its title and right even
when it errs in a political judgement and misuses its power. Etc.

Civil government, if it is to fulfill its office in the proper manner, must know
the moral-religious truth that is the light by which it must act. The Reformed
church considers it justified and called to know this. Civil government has a
clearly indicated and circumscribed terrain in which it is to act, and laboring in
and with the Word of God certainly does not pertain to it. The Reformed
church is certainly prepared to minister to civil government with the Word entrusted to the church, the Confession in which it summarizes that Word, and
the teaching that it provides in public. This cannot be said for Rome, but neither
can it be said for Kuyper's system.

Rome binds the government, which, as Brunetiére[130] said of late, has no
judgement of its own, to the judgement of the church. He who acts in accordance with its light, answers the question, "what do you believe?" with "ask
Rome!" And Dr. Kuyper binds it to *public opinion.* In principle this is exactly
the same thing and in practice it amounts to the same thing. The June 10th, 1900
issue of *The Herald* put it this way:

> The situation is factually this: in a nation, there forms a certain public opinion
> regarding the affairs of state and the obligations of the government; this opinion
> finds its expression in the laws and regulations; and the various civil servants are
> essentially bound by this.
>
> The will of God as revealed in nature and Scripture thus can become the rule
> and standard of the government's action in its various stages in no other way
> than by the confessors of the Lord, and especially the men of science among
> them, examining Scripture and demonstrating the principles of that Word in
> their application to the affairs of state. If in this way a powerful popular

---

[130] [Ferdinand Brunetière (1849–1906), a French free-thinker who became a conserva-
tive Catholic.]

conviction is formed, so that those who draft these laws bring these principles to expression, then the public course of business is bound to the will thus expressed....

We translate this as follows: if the Liberals are in power, then the laws will be Liberal, while if the Romish attain their goal, the laws will be Romish. Everything in the state revolves around the numerical or moral majority.

There are many objections to this way of viewing things:

1) It traps us in a vicious circle. Public opinion is to translate into legislation, but legislation hinders public opinion from coming to expression, and so forth.

2) It is either vain or dangerous. It is vain as long as the Lower House, or whatever other such entity, has not "turned" or, which amounts to the same thing, as often as a shrewd leader manages to profit from the errors and weakness of the opposition party. It is dangerous because it paves the way for the waxing influence of Rome, an influence that is all the more to be feared because Rome understands the art of profiting from every opportunity better than does internally-divided Protestantism, is not choosy about the means it uses, and knows how to take advantage of the self-interest, fear and weakness of any political party.

3) It kills the church by separation and schism, paralyzes the nerve of the people by political calculation, runs directly counter to the demand of faith by which one is to seek his strength not in the great mass but in the truth and in the God of truth, and shifts the center of gravity away from the church to the school and the university.

4) It can tear down, but it cannot build up.

The objection which lies at the root of all other objections lies in the Revolutionary, Romish conception that makes the government into an executive robbed of faith, understanding, and conscience, carrying out that which someone else has thought out.

3. THE STATE WITH THE BIBLE

The gravamen tabled in 1896 in Middelburg is not as benign as it looks. It deals with more than just the question of how the civil government is to deal with heretics as understood by the article in question of our Confession; indeed, with all kinds of questions connected to this, regarding the knowledge of God, the church, Holy Scripture, interpretation of Scripture, the relation of the Old and New Covenants, etc. And the system into which the gravamen fits, in terms of its leading idea, is, as our fathers would say, libertine, i.e., the opposite of anti-revolutionary.

How does all of this fit in with the recognized position of Dr. Kuyper and his supporters on theological-ecclesiastical terrain, and with the struggle that Dr. Kuyper for years has conducted against "unbelief and revolution," even if in a manner not always acceptable to us?

For the answer, we borrow material from issue no. 1192 of *The Herald.* The writer here tells us that the Roman Catholics lodge the same complaint against the Protestants that he gets lodged against him, when he is called a neutralist. The Catholics equate the Revolution and the Reformation. He writes,

If *you* do not shrink before this accusation, neither will you terrorize *us* with the bogeyman of neutrality, as long as any further evidence is lacking.

Where lies the difference between us and the sons of the Revolution?

They derive the structure of human life from the expression of human will, deny the revelation of God's will, declare all faith to be a matter of indifference, make science rooted in unbelief to be the judge of the life questions of the day, and are neutral in the bad sense of the word. Their neutrality is anti-clerical and has its origin in animosity.

Our aim is precisely to throw up a barrier against the Revolution. We consider all state interference to be harmful.

These things are not unknown to us. No one can or would want to cast into doubt what Dr. Kuyper here writes regarding his aim. True, one might have something to say about his argument in *The Herald*. Dr. Kuyper's "as long as any further evidence is lacking" could elicit a sharp response. His claim "we do not deny the revelation of God's will" would provide the opportunity to note that the distinction between such a denial and the position "the government would need a supernatural organ to understand God's will" in practice is not so great.

Furthermore, we would have opportunity to note that good intentions not only cannot save us, but harbor a unique danger for those to whom they are attributed and who rely on them, as well as for those of us whose fundamental objections are shunted aside by them. Jehoshaphat became allied by marriage with Ahab. He did so with the best of intentions. He sought to bring the rule of the divided kingdom into one hand. With just as good intentions, Josiah intervened in the struggle between Babylon and Egypt. But because of what Jehoshaphat did for his people, David's house would have been eradicated had God not prevented it. And Josiah died at Megiddo, and his kingdom fell.

More Errors in Kuyper's System

Besides the errors already mentioned, three mistakes underlie Dr. Kuyper's system:

1) It demands of the modern state, which purports to be neutral, that it not take sides and so facilitate the application of a positive Christian principle... and thus presumes even the possibility of a right of existence for neutrality which could benefit the Christian-Protestant principle.

2) It makes use of the power of the party, the coalition, in connection with the ballot box, to thwart the power of liberalism in its quest to make its principles predominant in church and school... but forgets that the weapons it puts to use in this struggle are those by which unbelief and superstition gained supremacy in the first place.

3) It transfers the struggle from political to social terrain... but hereby gets stuck in this vicious circle: the power of the state is needed to transform society, while society is needed to change the state.

We are struck with paralysis from the moment that the demand that the government bow before the revealed will of God is exchanged for the goal of *Our Program,* "to develop the keynote of our popular character, as stamped by the influence of the Reformation under the leadership of the House of Orange, in agreement with the changed popular condition, in a form which answers to the requirements of our time."[131]

Have we, that is to say, has not our people visibly declined in every respect? Our resilience is paralyzed, our church divided, the national character of the Christian school is lost, the center of gravity of movement has shifted from the church to "the association for higher education," "the Central Committee," "Patrimonium [Christian labor union]," in a word, to the ballot box, the ideal of our living and striving has vanished! When the apostle Paul stood on the Areopagus and gained a few adherents for the truth he proclaimed, he was addressing the people as a whole. But according to Kuyper's system, on the cardinal issues we act in the interest of a group, an institute, an association.

If the church concept that one seeks to apply is true, if the calculations prove accurate, then this approach promises outstanding results.... But, we have withdrawn within more restricted circles and limited our horizon to the interests or presumed interests of our supporters.

This is a highly dangerous method:

1) because it makes the goal relative.

Of course, we cannot be so doctrinaire that we neglect to take existing conditions into account and try to take advantage of them. In the assembly of the Jewish council, the apostle Paul appealed to the Pharisees against the Sadducees because the latter would have done him the most evil at that point in time.

If we are to rebuild, renovate the dilapidated house, we must in the meantime put up supports for the roof and hang tarpaulin to make the drafty rooms habitable, because there is need of shelter. If the resident does not first take heed

---

[131] *Our Program,* Article 1.

for his own body, the improvement that he hopes to obtain by rebuilding the house will be of no use to him.

While all of this is true, one is still faced with a dilemma, for it all depends on *the object* of the intended restorations. If one seeks in this way to maintain what is not viable, then cooperation in the realization of this desire can backfire.

2) Because it estranges the church and Christendom from the living movement of the times.

Those who champion a bland Protestantism, who do not go to church, who desire a Christendom without Christian content, who are at peace with a church without discipline and science without principle: it lies in the nature of the case that they will reject the demand of *Our Program*. But those who desire something more positive, something Scriptural, in agreement with our Confession, for them the temptation to follow Dr. Kuyper's method is great. They are in agreement with what he writes. He only expresses what they feel.... In all of this there is only one *but*. The ideal can only be realized through kindred spirits, and for their benefit. And this little group, reduced by the pressure of this principle, is ecclesiastically isolated, while society either becomes more and more secularized or is delivered over to Rome.

The Road to Recovery

The gains from this method do not outweigh the losses! We can quickly achieve the immediate goal. But by doing so we lose the church and the people!

We consider the ideal that Article 1 of *Our Program* presents to be an illusion, and we demand, on the basis of his own Confession, that Dr. Kuyper and his followers either return to the truth which lies at the intersection of all possible deviations and differences, or provide the evidence that Article 36, in which this truth is partly expressed, partly presupposed, is in conflict with the Word of God.

It concerns all the church for all the people; the honor of God; the union of confessors; the recovery of strength and right.

We gladly absolve the brothers who departed from the national church, who act in terms of the method we have rejected, once and for all of the accusation that they consciously comported with unbelief and superstition. But we cannot absolve them of the pursuit to struggle against them while neglecting the church and the Confession, instead resorting to the school and the political organization. That will not work. It is in conflict with God's Word and God's way. God put the church in the middle of the life of the people. Is it possible to rip the heart that has become sick from out of the body, and bring about a localized healing that did not come about through the normal way of blood circulation? Neglect the breathing and nutrimental organs, remove the heart from the body, and hope to maintain the sick person along purely mechanical lines, but do not expect to maintain the sick society, and the state corresponding to it, apart from the organ through which God pleases to live and work in the world.

The first step on the road to the Reformation is the recovery of the normal relations of church and state. As soon as one realizes this, there awakens in him the zeal that otherwise slumbers.

In one of the articles in *The Herald* to which we have already referred, the acknowledgement is made that those to whom the writer refers as "the Reformed" [Nonconformists] do not desire a Reformed civil government. This pronouncement did not surprise us. It only expresses what we already sensed and stated in another context, the ecclesiastical: secret fear of the Reformed church, a fear which hinders true reformation in church and state. As we asked in *All the Church for All the People:*

> Do you believe that God can once again make the Netherlands a Christian nation, the government of the Netherlands a Christian government, the Dutch Reformed church a properly ordered church? Do you believe that He in His own time shall do it? Do you wish that He would do this; would you consider it a blessing if He did do this; are you convinced that we are lost if He does not do this?
>
> Generally speaking, people do *not* want this. They gladly keep going along the accustomed path.[132]

Erroneous ideas about freedom of religion

We should add that this state of public opinion, not among the *opponents*, mind you, but among the *friends* of truth, is the consequence of erroneous

---

[132] *Heel de Kerk voor Heel het Volk* (Sneek: J. Campen, 1897), p. 19.

imaginings which have been formed regarding church and state as we understand it. As long as people are unconvinced that the recovery of which we speak would be a blessing for our nation and people, and seek to gain others to this conviction, no power can proceed from us to achieve the intended goal.

But for this reason it is of the utmost necessity to achieve clarity on this point.

We wrote as follows[133] in response to Dr. Kuyper's claim cited above:

> Our times lack the gift of discernment, which is why error has such an easy time gaining a foothold. We fear the application of Reformed principles because we do not, or, if we do, we only barely distinguish between freedom of conscience and freedom of religion, equate it with the freedom to propagandize for our notions, equate this freedom with the freedom to slander, and confuse these four kinds of freedom with the theory of the Revolution, that the civil government as such may have no conviction, which is the reason why it may not recognize any church as the true one.[134]

"Christ alone is the Lord of conscience," said the High Mightinesses in the placard of 1619, providing the assurance that no one in this country would be molested because of his opinions on religion.

It is in conflict with history when the matter is so presented as if there were a pagan viewpoint which was first taken over by the Roman church, then by Protestantism, and which subsequently, gradually was supplanted by a more

---

[133] *The Reformed Church,* July 16th, 1891.

[134] Our fathers used to make a distinction between: *libertas a coactione* [freedom from coercion]; *libertas conscientiae, conniventia* or *tolerantia religionis* [freedom of conscience, connivance or tolerance of religion]; *libertas religionis*, i.e., *lib. relig. ad omnia et singula exercitia tum publica tum privata* [the exercise of the freedom of religion directed to all and to the individual, both public and private]; *libertas habitationis* [freedom of domicile]; *libertas blasphemandi* [freedom to commit blasphemy]. *Synopsis Purioris Theologiae* (Leyden: Elsevier, 1625), Disp. L. LIX. William Ames, *Conscience with the Power and Cases Thereof* (London: n.p., 1639), Book IV, ch. III. Voetius, *Polit. Eccl.,* 1.401.

liberal sense and greater generosity. We already knew the reason behind not forcing faith or promoting it by fear and hope. This was the direct, obvious consequence that could be derived from the Confession itself.

The *Synopsis* expressed it this way:

Although the magistrate may prohibit his subjects from publicly slandering the religion that he approves, he may not obligate them to accept faith, i.e., the form of confession approved by public right, and to confess and render assurance of this before men. Faith arises through persuasion, not coercion. People should be left more to their own devices about religion than about anything else. The Christian magistrate must avoid nothing as much as the foolish, impetuous severity which nurtures hypocrites, and forces subjects to confess with their mouths without believing in their hearts.[135]

In agreement with this, Ames wrote:

Ques. 9. Whether ought Infidels to be compelled to the profession of the true Faith by such as be their governours?

14 A.1. They ought not to be compelled to it. 1. Because Faith itself cannot be wrought by constraint. The act of true Faith proceeds always from a free will, not from feare or force, Psal. 47 10. Acts 2.41. 2. Because externall profession without internall Faith, is nothing but hypocrisie. 3. Because the Church by this meanes is corrupted, whilst those are thrust upon it as members which are not fit.[136]

Yet freedom of religion is something entirely different from freedom of conscience.

According to our Confession, the civil government is to determine

1) which *religion* in the state is to be accepted into the commonwealth and as such is to be protected and administered with public authority;

2) which religion will be allowed and tolerated.

---

[135] *Synopsis Purioris Theologiae* [Synopsis of a Purer Theology] Disp. L. LIX.

[136] Ames, *Conscience with the Power and Cases Thereof,* Book IV, ch. III, p. 9.

The "removal and prevention of heresy and false religion" of which the Confession speaks, therefore has nothing to do with Christian churches and sects separated from each other in this way or that, but with entirely different groups which, through their godless positions or what our fathers considered to be such, infringe on the honor of God. It *presupposes the freedom discussed above*, which is inseparable from the national Reformed church's viewpoint regarding faith and the work of the Holy Spirit.

The expression just quoted therefore not only can but must be restricted to *public life*, the sphere to be reckoned to the civil government.

Is blasphemy to be tolerated?

Even after taking into account these restrictions, which are of the nature of the case, another distinction is to be made between two cases pertaining to this rubric. In the one case, the civil government's duty to do so is absolute, leaving no room for negotiation, while in the other, the state and public interest should be taken into account.

The former case is that of the blasphemer and idolator, the latter is that of the heretic, who in the eyes of our fathers – leaving aside the question of whether they saw rightly or not – holds to soul-killing, God-dishonoring error.

This distinction shows that the opinion of Dr. Kuyper and his followers indeed does not differ from that of our fathers regarding the treatment of grave heretics and blasphemers.

After all, the civil government's obligation to act with coercive power against all blasphemy where it directly takes the character of contumely against God's majesty, is something that not even Dr. Kuyper rejects.

And as regards blasphemy, the right of the magistrate to restrain it rests in the God-consciousness innate in every man; and the duty to exercise this right flows from the fact that God is the Supreme and Sovereign Ruler over every State and over every Nation. But for this very reason the fact of blasphemy is only then to be deemed established, when the intention is apparent contumaciously to affront this majesty of God as Supreme Ruler of the State. What is then punished is not the religious offence, nor the impious sentiment, but the attack upon the foundation of public law, upon which both the State and its government are resting.[137]

Please allow us in passing to note that the writer has apparently forgotten how indignant he was when others "had him saying" that the civil government is not bound to the revelation of God's will in Holy Scripture. He has returned to his old love for the natural knowledge of God in the terrain of politics. But this and whatever else is disconcerting in the conception put forward here ought not hinder us from acknowledging that the gentlemen who tendered the gravamen at Middelburg apparently were mistaken in holding that they were *in disagreement* with our Reformers in what they put forward. There can be differences in the judgement as to whether this or that expression, for example, the name "three-headed dog of hell," which Servetus gave to the Trinity, truly is to be considered blasphemy or just "an honorable expression of an opinion that deviates from ours," but there is no difference regarding the question as to *whether blasphemy is actually punishable* or not.

As appears from the quotation from the *Lectures on Calvinism,* Dr. Kuyper has defined blasphemy within such narrow bounds that we truly do not know *which* "annoying and disrespectful manifestations of a wandering mind and a hostile heart" could be categorized as such. But this is not to the point.

What is to the point is the clarification that our fathers gave to the offending clause in the well-known article of our Confession, not as *The Herald* has it, "gradually as morals became somewhat milder," but from the start and immediately after the days of the Reformation, whereby they drew a clear distinction between purposeful blasphemy and blasphemy which was not so intended by the speaker or writer but was only considered to be so by readers or hearers. This is precisely what Dr. Kuyper is concerned with.

After all, blasphemy in the objective and restricted sense must always and under all circumstances be punished. "Religion," said Rivetus, "should not be tempered by politics, but the reverse, by God's Word."[138]

---

[137] *Lectures on Calvinism,* p. 103.

[138] [No source given.]

And furthermore, no one can have disposal over another's right. It is God's right to be honored by His creatures, independent of all possible circumstances. Blasphemy is a crime, just as murder is, and is its equivalent. But there were forms of heresy and false religion which the civil government under certain conditions could and should tolerate, when the constitution so required. As often as acquired rights were to be respected. In that case, the strict measures against heretics maintained in this country might redound against our fellow believers elsewhere, so that they might be persecuted by way of retaliation. In case of danger of domestic disturbances. Or if the evil was too deeply rooted to be removed in this manner. "Remove and prevent" was thus a matter of policy.[139]

The magistrate must keep the religion that he sanctions from being slandered.[140]

One question remains, whether Servetus truly belonged among the blasphemers who are punishable by Dr. Kuyper's standard. By way of answer, the following quotation from Trigland is sufficient:

> The Remonstrants, keeping silent about Servetus' abominations, only report what serves to foster pity. Can everything be stewed in the kettle of the history writer? — or is the language Servetus uses not blasphemy? If not, then there is no blasphemy in the world.... Yes, but some say to kill a man for his opinions is a bit harsh. The opinion concerns God, not men! One might rightly respond by saying that it is not so much the opinion that is the important thing as the slanderous speeches made with the mouth against God.[141]

In one of the council hearings led by Calvin, he noted that Servetus' doctrine not only overthrew Christianity but religion generally, making no distinction between Creator and creature.

---

[139] *Synopsis Purioris Theologiae,* Disp. L. LV. [This paragraph renders the gist of that section, but it appears to be conflated with another, unmentioned source.]

[140] *Ibid.,* Disp. L. LIX.

[141] Jacobus Trigland, *Kerckelycke geschiedenissen* [Ecclesiastical Histories] (Leyden: Adriaen Wyngaerden, 1650), vol II, p. 117.

"Of course," responded Servetus with a contemptuous chuckle, "God lives as much in the devil as in the floor."

"What, wretch!" cried Calvin, leaping up startled, full of dismay, "does one step on the Deity when he places his feet on this floor? You must be ashamed to relate this nonsense."

"On the contrary," replied Servetus, "that this floor, or whatever you point out to me, is of the essence of God is absolutely certain."

When Calvin and all the Reformers are condemned because they called "blasphemy" what in the eyes of our exceedingly humane, extremely fair-minded and eager to justify, peace-loving contemporaries is only a difference of opinion, a reading of Servetus' chief works and the council hearings will disabuse them of this notion. The distinction between blasphemy in the objective and the subjective sense is in his case eliminated. His doctrine that no essential distinction existed between good and evil, God and Satan, filled the men who had put their lives on the line for the truth with horror. But it will be difficult for those who neither understand nor share their emotion to acquit the form in which he presented this doctrine of "all suspicion of blasphemy." Expressions like "three-headed dog of hell," "excrement of Satan," appear on every page of his work.[142] Speaking of those who call Christ the Son of God, he wrote "they must either accept that God has a spiritual wife, or that He must be a manwoman."[143]

"If the Son is born of a father without a mother, tell me how He was given birth, from the belly or from the side?"[144]

It does us no honor to hear such language with such calm and resignation!

The same holds true for the abominations in the Roman church. It will not hurt us to renew our acquaintance with the opinions of our fathers. Read, for example, the "Day of Prayer Petition" of 1624 by Cornelis Huygens, who in his confession of national sins expressed himself thusly about Rome:

---

[142] M. Servetus, *de Trinitatis Erroribus* [On the Errors of the Trinity] J. Calvinus, *In Serveti Refutationem* [Refutation of Servet] Theod. Beza, *de Hereticis a Magistratu puniendis* [On the Punishment of Heretics by the Magistrate].

[143] *De Trinit. Error.* I, pag. 16.

[144] *Ibid.*, II, pag. 52.

> They are the more guilty
> who more than half smother
> the full merit of His only-begotten,
> and brag as if the guilt
> were more than satisfied
> by her payments
> More, who leave the one path
> of way, truth, and life
> in an idolatrous manner,
> And seek in need,
> Life in death,
> in powerless bones.

But precisely from this it appears all the more that our fathers both made the distinction in blasphemy in the above-mentioned sense, and had a different reason for not extending "freedom of religion" in the fullest sense of the word to the adherents of this religion.

Jacobus Fruytier rejected the opinion put forward by the Puritans but likewise rejected by our divines, that the texts of the Old Testament which demanded the death penalty for priests of Baal, should be applied to Papists.

The Canaanites were under the ban. Israel, on the other hand, was God's possession out of all the peoples of the earth, they had laws that do not now bind the people of the Lord. Nowhere is the Christian commanded to banish, rob, torment, or kill for the sake of religion. We should not teach that which we condemn in them. It is the Netherlands' glory that no one is molested for the sake of religion. Many Papists shook off the Spanish yoke, just as we did, and fought for the freedom of the Netherlands. But it does not follow that their idolatrous religion should be freely exercised everywhere, that their boldnesses should be endured.[145]

Udemans argued against the public exercise of the Papist religion on, among others, the following ground:

Fifth. The basic rules of the Roman church are such that they do not make oath-breaking a matter of conscience when it benefits them to do so, for the advantage (so they say) of the Romish religion (Council of Constance, session 19). For this reason, Prince William of Nassau of blessed memory said in his Apology, fol. 67, that although the States of the United Provinces from the beginning of the war until the preservation of the nation, found it good and useful to maintain different religions, nevertheless later on, due to the wantonness, shrewd practices, and betrayals of the enemies, were warned that their State was facing the danger of ultimate ruin unless they suspended and prohibited the exercise of the Roman religion, because those who made profession of the same, swore another oath to the Pope, which they considered to be superior to that which they swore to the Fatherland.[146]

The Pope presumes to possess the highest authority on Earth, the right to set up and dismiss kings, the competence to determine good and evil. He wishes to be a secular lord, release citizens from their obligation to the civil government, attack by virtue of his persuasion not only religion but also freedom of conscience, and undermine by the same persuasion the foundation of our civil freedom. For these and similar reasons, our fathers restricted the freedom of the Romish religion and excluded them from government.

In the preface to his *De Summo Pontifice*, Bellarmine asks, "what is at issue in this conflict regarding the primacy of the Pope? I can say it in one word: it is the highest interest of Christianity (*de summa rei christianae*). At issue is the question of whether the church will continue to stand or fall.... If the Pope

---

[145] Jacobus Fruytier, *Gerigtshandelingen van den allerhoogsten God met Zijn volk in Nederland* [Acts of judgement of the Most High God with His people in the Netherlands], 5th ed. (Utrecht: J. J. H. Kemmer, 1860), vol I, p. 315.

[146] Udemans, *'t Geestelyck roer van 't coopmans schip*, p. 312.

could err and support vice, abolish virtue, the church would be obligated to believe that good is evil and evil good, unless it wished to sin against conscience."

We need add nothing to this – or only what Pope Leo X wrote about marriage on June 1ˢᵗ, 1879:

"Outside the forms established by God and the church, marriage is neither honorable nor holy. The ecclesiastical act is no blessing of a marriage consummated by the civil government, no appendage, but the only way in which marriage can be legally consummated."

This is comprehensible language. He who has ears to hear, let him hear! But there is something that keeps us from drawing the obvious conclusion from this and other objectionable doctrines held by the Roman church, namely, that against the anti-revolutionaries and in the interest of the liberals it would be ascribed to anti-papal ferocity.

This is not about one political party in distinction from the others, but about the foundational principle of the modern state and against the attempt to realize a majority at the ballot box through coalition with the goal of putting in the service of God's cause what the Revolution brought to the terrain of the state. The neutral state benefits Rome; and the liberals, except when they are making their otherwise inadequate arguments against Rome, are its natural allies. Those who wish to be Reformed in statecraft only have to demand that the civil government rule according to God's Word, that civil government have its vocation stipulated in the constitution under the guarantees of the freedom of the people, and that this be done in the only form in which civil government can bind itself to an ecclesiastical confession, namely, by recognizing that the church purified of error is a *matter of public right*.

The Reformed standpoint has nothing to with the petty application of an entirely different principle, which at bottom is pagan, namely, that of a state religion and a ruling church, which was combatted by our fathers.

We do not understand why the state cannot make use of the *bona fide* services of Jews and Catholics, as long as it does not do so because of their being Jews or Catholics, and with the proviso that the abuse of their position and influence in the service of error will be guarded against. We do not see why the people as an entirety should not be allowed to promote its interests in the assembly of representatives. If the form of government allows, that is, if – and this is the point of contention – the boundary between government and popular representation is not erased.[147]

Free Church versus Church by Public Right

But it is high time to turn the tables. The accused now has the right to act as prosecutor.

What is this babbling about a free church in a free state? It is precisely the characteristic of the Revolution that it does *not* allow the church to be itself. Every being on God's earth has the right to be what God made it to be, and may demand of the state that it (the state) not hinder it from doing its duty. But in both respects the Revolution has infringed on the church.

This state recognizes three relations to moral persons:

1) Associations of individuals brought together to pursue a specific goal. Without a determinate form, exclusively local, and for a determinate time period. Such associations are granted legal personality by the state, which only inquires as to whether members have influence on the composition of the managerial board, whether there is an arrangement for ordered departures, and the like. It does not bother with the goal of the cooperative effort.

2) Foundations with a more enduring character, independent of their bylaws, in possession of goods with a specific purpose, a purpose namely not for the persons bringing those goods together, but for posterity, i.e., the goal of the foundation in successive generations.

3) Associations spread out over various locations with local departments all of which have managing boards under a general board that represents the association at law. Until 1797–1798, state documents spoke of the "church;" thereafter, they spoke of "denominations" [kerkgenootschappen], describing them as associations "for the exercise and promotion of religion."

---

[147] [A reference to constitutional monarchy, in which government (under the monarch) and representation remain separate: see also pp. 62, 63 above. For details on this system of government, see Friedrich Julius Stahl, *The Doctrine of State and the Principles of State Law* (Aalten: WordBridge, 2010), ch. 12, "The Monarchical Principle," pp. 275ff.]

In the draft bill of 1797 Article 10, the church congregations are labelled associations [genootschappen]. It has here to do with "associations pertaining to the indicated privileged church." But soon thereafter, the meaning of the word shifts from an association of (local) churches to a church which is an association of persons – and the local churches disappear as entities. The law only recognizes departments with boards under a single administrative board joined into one association.

In terms of its origin and character, the church is not an association bound by the expression of the will of its members for a certain goal, nor an association the departments and members of which have no independent existence and no rights that they do not obtain from the central board, but a *revelation of the body of Christ* which as such is visible locally and is completely autonomous regarding everything that can be accomplished locally. Nor is it contractually bound to all other local churches, but is bound to them by virtue of the unity of origin and goal, life and effort, Head and law, and acts as a unity either in more restricted circles, classical or provincial, or in more extended ones, national and international, so that the individual is bound to the consistory and the consistories to more extended assemblies, and subjected to them by virtue of the composition of power.[148]

What did the Revolution accomplish? Not only did it deny the church all lawful influence on the state, but it forced the church to take on a form which not only is alien to its life but which denies its supernatural origin. After all, it follows from the standpoint taken by the state that the origin of the moral person, in this case the denomination, flows from the state, i.e., from its authorization,[149] and is dependent upon the will of its members for its existence and manner of action.[150]

---

[148] [For a full exposition, see Hoedemaker, *Reformed Ecclesiology in an Age of Denominationalism.*]

[149] *The Reformed Church,* no. 13.

[150] The fact that this is not benign appears from the treatment given the national Reformed church in France. In 1803 the Protestant churches in France received official

We have arrived here at the core of the bone of contention between us and the Liberals, along with the Anti-Revolutionaries and affiliated orientations.

Here again it is the story repeated in a variety of forms of the stone rejected by the builders being made by God into the cornerstone.

The Revolution will only be combatted with success when we do not ourselves take a standpoint in the Revolution. Those who left the national church in 1886 are completely in the right when they reject the existence of the national church as a denomination. But they forget, firstly, that although the church and the offices are forced into this framework, they still exist in their actual essence,[151] and secondly, that it is not any better to allow the church to vanish in terms of state law. This is a denial of Christ with regard to civil government.

The Separation, the Nonconformity, the sad situation in which the national church finds itself, are a consequence of the incongruous relation between church and state. Should the church – this is the question at the heart of all possible questions – should the church just withdraw from public life and seek shelter in small separated congregations which the state leaves in peace? The answer can and must be *no* and only no.

---

recognition but the law of *12 Germinal an X* makes no mention of a synod. The churches continued to insist on the restoration of the previous organization, but it took until 1872 before Jules Simon allowed them to call a synod. At this synod, which met in Paris, the church split into an orthodox and a modernist wing. The modernists removed themselves and the government refused to attach its approval to the decisions taken. The orthodox decided to come together in an unofficial assembly, the decisions of which had no compelling power. The *Figaro* of June 8th, 1896 states that the orthodox "should not think that their synod is the harbinger of an official national synod.... The government is bound and determined to keep itself from any interference in church affairs (!).... This could be an occasion to establish peace, because for those who remain in the church, coercion of conscience will in no way be the consequence (!)."

[151] Dr. Ph. J. Hoedemaker, *De Congresbeweging beoordeeld uit het oogpunt der gereformeerde belijdenis* [The Congress Movement judged from the perspective of the Reformed confession] (Amsterdam: J. A. Wormser, 1887).

What is at stake here is not the right of the church, but the right and the honor of God. The struggle against the Revolution is concentrated on the question, whether the civil government, and in a constitutional state, the constitution, will extend a public-legal existence to the church as the revelation of the body of Christ.

Dr. Kuyper quite properly formulated this demand.[152]

We only object to

1) his putting the church on the same level as the other spheres (family, art, school) all of which he says are "of public right," and according to his doctrine of "sphere sovereignty," would give a jurisdiction independent of the state;

2) his attributing to the state no independent judgement, but assumes that it has to reserve to the church what presents itself as such and in the way in which such presents itself;

3) the state having to recognize and listen to *all* churches, i.e., in the terminology of the fathers, both the true and the false church; to which end he wishes to establish – seriously now! – an "advisory council."

If this notion were to be realized, the proverb "this people perishes because of a multitude of counsellors" would be applicable.

To ask the question is to answer it.

All right, then, show us!

The church acts in accordance with the confession that the Word of God is entrusted to it, that the Holy Spirit who leads it into all truth dwells in it, and that it is called by God to be a pillar and foundation of the truth, and to administer the Word of God. The question to which the civil government must give an answer is this: shall I recognize this entity that comes to me "in the name of the Lord," or shall I reject it; shall I enable it to fulfill its vocation, or pay no

---

[152] "That same God who set up the government, and invested the government with authority as His servant, that same God brought the church of Christ into this world by virtue of His sovereign supreme power, and dispersed it over all nations and peoples. That church is not a product of human will or deed, but a creation of God. It is therefore not asked of the government whether it will admit that church... it exists *iure divino*." It cannot be better said. A step further... acknowledge that God gave shape to that church... and thou art where thou ought to be.

attention to it; listen to it and, when necessary, consult it, or go my way as if Christ was not put in the world to be Lord of all? The answer to this question is confirmed when the state maintains the church as *of public right*; denied, when, for the state, the church is either a club, or a foundation, or an association. After all, these are purely human institutions, while the church is a divine-human institution.

The church does not fit into the framework the state has prepared for it. Only the Word of God teaches what it is. If the question is put purely, all of this is not amenable to contradiction. It lies in the nature of the case.

But it follows from this that the state cannot maintain two or more churches as of public right, as little as two Christs. It can admit many churches and allow them to act and to labor, but there is only one church the confession of which is "publicly implemented and protected." The consequence cannot be avoided unless one denies that the government is bound to the revealed will of God, i.e., God's Word.[153]

It is necessary to define the boundaries of the state.

The state is not authorized to give public interpretation of the Word, i.e., it is not to provide a confession and catechism ... but it may and must judge which confession it will put at the foundation of legislation and public policy.

Not only this. It is to consult the church in all cases that come up.

Should one wish "to keep the church out of it," if one separates the church from the state, there are only three conceivable options: either the state has its own religion elevated above divisions of faith, or it becomes an atheist state and eliminates everything Christian from all public institutions, or it leaves legislation to chance, i.e., the momentary majority.

The standpoint we here take, that of our Confession, is commonly disparaged as "counter-revolutionary." No wonder. The same reproach was directed at Groen van Prinsterer in his time. Do you know how he responded? "Nous ne voulons pas le contre revolution, mais le contraire de la Revolution!" [We are not the counter-revolution, but the opposite of the Revolution.]

---

[153] [Hoedemaker proffers another solution in *Reformed Ecclesiology in an Age of Denominationalism,* where he opens the prospect of a conciliar solution on the basis of a frank acceptance of pluriformity.]

In this sense there is a confusion of tongues. Many who allow the church to vanish from the terrain of the state, confer upon political and educational associations the church's vocation to expound the Word, consider the Word of God to be a closed book for civil government, and call themselves anti-revolutionary simply because they oppose the objective of the Liberals on dogmatic, ecclesiastical, or social terrain.

Let us not dispute about names and words. Just know this: one does not derive the right to call himself anti-revolutionary from the rejection of something characteristic that the Revolution effectuated in the state, not even, to a certain degree, popular sovereignty,[154] but only if, by doing so, he hopes to realize his ideals in ecclesiastical, social, and educational terrain and *in so doing* combats the unbelief from which the Revolution derived.

The homeopathic method on political terrain!

Groen van Prinsterer demanded that the public school not introduce a watered-down, impure Christianity. He was brought to this by the fear that the modernist-sectarian school might de-christianize the nation. And those who continue in this line call themselves the heirs of Groen's principle, leaving aside for the moment whether they do so rightly or wrongly.

But the same confusion is here at work. It is one Groen who unfolds his system of state law, and another who acts as leader of a group among the people and in the Lower House. The first Groen, who demands "State reform in the fatherland sense, and constitutional reform in the Dutch sense," is the Groen whom we put forward as spokesman and advocate of the principles contrary to those of *The Herald*.

We use his words to express our desire:[155]

The state law that I recommend, rejecting the state law by which God is excluded from the state, is inseparably joined to religion. Authority, law, and

---

[154] See n. 147.

[155] *Bijdrage tot herziening der Grondwet in Nederlandschen zin* [Contribution to the revision of the constitution in the Dutch sense] (Leyden: S. and J. Luchtmans, 1840), pp. 65–66, 71–72, 73.

freedom are not conventional but traditional, are independent of human approval or disapproval, and are grounded in God's will and essence.

It is historical, which is to say, it agrees with man and nature; it is built on the essence of law and state: an ideal, but one in which an ongoing realization is found in history. It is the opposite of revolutionary state law, which is merely imaginary, based on what is not, on untruths and fantastic concepts....

And when it is asked how this state law managed to manifest itself and develop in the Netherlands, with respect to the present moment, I believe I may say:

The Netherlands was not founded in the revolution of 1795, nor by the constitutions of 1814 or 1815; it is a historic state, in which revolutionary arrogance was unable to destroy all freedoms and rights.

The Netherlands is a Christian nation, in which regard for the gospel is the right and duty of civil government and subject. The civil government, Christian or not, must maintain this highest law of the land.

The Netherlands is a Protestant state, in which, along with more expansive toleration, the maintenance and interest of the Christian-Protestant church must be provided for.

The Netherlands is a country in which monarchical authority has long existed, and in which, even during the Republic, the tendency toward monarchy, as toward the guarantee against local oppression, specifically the desire for the House of Orange, was national.

The Netherlands is a free country, in which the rights of particular persons and corporations of all kinds are honored, and the nation had an important influence on affairs of state, as often as it was not subjected to the yoke of the aristocrats.

The bare showing of these main characteristics will, I flatter myself, reassure those who fear that the orientation toward these principles is insufficiently practical.

And this:

The gospel is the precious inheritance of the nation.

The point is not outward appearances, fine words and testimonies, a billboard, a holy state like once the holy covenant; not the weaving into an act of state a tribute to the loving administration of a wise Providence; not, in the name of violating the Sabbath, punishment of the hungry laborer seeking bread for his family while allowing all manner, not merely of amusement, but of immorality. No, we desire something more. The national faith is the Christian faith, the national education is Christian education, the national legislation is Christian legislation. Therefore, an equality may no longer be forced upon us in the Netherlands by which revelation is made equal to the Koran and the Zend Avesta; an education with pagan moral doctrine as its foundation; a penal law only taking the utility and the security of society into account, rather than maintaining God's honor and His general prescriptions.

Finally, this:

Even though there is no ruling church, even though the various faith communities that used to be tolerated now exist by acquired right, we must either continually accept the ungodliness of the law, something the corruption of which is felt by all Christian faith communities, or, if there is a historic state, then by the nature of the case the Reformed church as the national church.

APPENDIX

The Herald issue number	Common Grace (vol. 3) ch. no.	"Church and State" series no.	Date
1140	1		29 October 1899
1141	2		5 November 1899
1142	3		12 November 1899
1143	4		19 November 1899
1144	5		26 November 1899
1145	6		3 December 1899
1146	7		10 December 1899
1147	8		17 December 1899
1148			24 December 1899
1149			31 December 1899
1150	9		7 January 1900
1151	10		14 January 1900
1152	11		21 January 1900
1153	12		28 January 1900
1154	13	1	4 February 1900
1155	14	2	11 February 1900
1156	15	3	18 February 1900
1157	16	4	25 February 1900
1158	17	5	4 March 1900
1159	18	6	11 March 1900
1160	19	7	18 March 1900
1161	20	8	25 March 1900
1162	21	9	1 April 1900
1163	22	10	8 April 1900
1164			15 February 1900
1165	23	11	22 April 1900
1166	24	12	29 April 1900

1167			5 May 1900
1168	25[156]	13	13 May 1900
1169	26	14	27 May 1900
1170			3 June 1900
1171	27	15	10 June 1900
1172	28	16	17 June 1900
1173	29	17	24 June 1900
1174	30	18	1 July 1900
1175	31	19	8 July 1900
1176			15 July 1900
1177			22 July 1900
1178			29 July 1900
1179			5 August 1900
1180			12 August 1900
1181			19 August 1900
1182			26 August 1900
1183			2 September 1900
1184			9 September 1900
1185	32	20	16 September 1900
1186	33	21	23 September 1900
1187	34	22	30 September 1900
1188	35	23	7 October 1900
1189	36	24	14 October 1900
1190	37	25	21 October 1900
1191	38	26	28 October 1900
1192	39	27	4 November 1900
1193	40	28	11 November 1900

---

[156] Mistakenly published as ch. 24 in the original newspaper version.

REFERENCES

Ames, William. *Bellarminus enervatus*. Amsterdam: Ioannum Ianssonium, 1630.

—. *Conscience with the Power and Cases Thereof*. London, 1639.

Bellarmine, Robert. *Opera Omnia*. Naples: Josephum Giuliano, 1836.

Brakel, Wilhelmus à. *The Christian's Reasonable Service*. Trans. Bartel Elshout. Grand Rapids, MI: Reformation Heritage Books, 1993 [1700].

de Bie, Jan Pieter and Jakob Loosjes. *Biographisch Woordenboek van Protestantische Godgeleerden in Nederland*. Vol. 4. 's-Gravenhage: Martinus Nijhoff, 1931.

Dr. Ph. J. Hoedemaker 1868–1908: Gedenkboek ter Gelegenheid van zijn 40-Jarige Ambtsbediening. Leyden: De Vlieger, 1908.

Fruytier, Jacobus. *Gerigtshandelingen van den allerhoogsten God met Zijn volk in Nederland*. Utrecht: J. J. H. Kemmer, 1860.

Groen van Prinsterer, Guillaume. *Bijdrage tot herziening der Grondwet in Nederlandschen zin*. Leyden: S. and J. Luchtmans, 1840.

—. *Groen van Prinsterer's Lectures on Unbelief and Revolution*. Trans. Harry van Dyke. Jordan Station: Wedge Publishing Foundation, 1989.

—. *Ongeloof en Revolutie*. 3rd. Amsterdam: H. A. van Bottenburg, 1903 [1847].

Herald, The. Amsterdam: Kon. Ned. Stoomdrukkerij, 1877–.

Hodge, Charles. *Systematic Theology*. Vol. I. New York: Scribner, Armstrong, and Co., 1873. 3 vols.

Hoedemaker, P. J. *De Congresbeweging beoordeeld uit het oogpunt der gereformeerde belijdenis*. Amsterdam: J. A. Wormser, 1887.

—. *Ééne Belijdenis? Eene ernstige vraag naar aanleiding van mijn aftreden als Hoogleeraar aan de Vrije Universiteit*. Amsterdam: J. H. Kruyt, 1887.

—. *Heel de Kerk voor Heel het Volk*. Sneek: J. Campen, 1897.

—. *Op het fondament der apostelen en profeten*. Utrecht: C. van Bentum, 1886.

—. *Reformed Ecclesiology in an Age of Denominationalism*. Aalten: Pantocrator Press, 2019.

Koenen, Hendrik Jakob. *Geschiedenis der Joden in Nederland*. Utrecht: C. van der Post, 1843.

Kuipers, Tjitze. *Abraham Kuyper: An Annotated Bibliography 1857–2010*. Leyden: Brill, 2011.

Kuyper, Abraham. *De Gemeene Gratie*. Kampen: J. H. Kok, 1902–1904.

—. *E Voto Dordraceno*. 4 vols. Amsterdam: J. A. Wormser, 1892.

—. *Encyclopædie der heilige godgeleerdheid*. 3 vols. Amsterdam: J. A. Wormser, 1894.

—. *Encyclopedia of Sacred Theology: Its Principles*. Trans. Rev. J. Hendrik de Vries. New York: Charles Scribner's Sons, 1898.

—. *Lectures on Calvinism*. Grand Rapids, MI: Wm. B. Eerdmans Publishing Co., 1931 [1898].

—. *Ons Program*. Amsterdam: J. H. Kruyt, 1879.

—. *Our Program*. Trans. Harry van Dyke. Bellingham, WA: Lexham Press, 2015.

Marck, Johannes à. *Het merch der christelijke godtsgeleertheit* . Amsterdam: Gerardus Borstius, 1705.

Moehler, John Adam. *Symbolism: or, Exposition of the Doctrinal Differences between Catholics and Protestants*. Trans. James Burton Robertson. New York: Edward Dunnigan, 1844.

Moor, Bernardinus de. *Commentarius Perpetuus in Johannes Marckii Compendium Theologiae Christianae Didactico-Elenchticum*. Leyden: Johannem Hasebroek, 1661.

—. *Continuous Commentary on Johannes Marckius' Didactico-Elenctic Compendium of Christian Theology*. Trans. Steven Dilday. Culpeper, VA: L & G Reformation Translation Center, 2014.

Musculus, Wolfgang. *Loci communes sacrae Theologiae*. Basel: Ioannem Hervagium, 1561.

Reformed Church, The. Sneek: J. Campen, 1888–.

Rotterdam, Arnoldus. *Zions Roem en Sterkte ofte Verklaring van de Zevenendertig Artikelen der Nederlandsche Geloofs-Belydenis*. 2 vols. Amsterdam, Utrecht: Esveldt, van Vucht, Paddenburg, 1755.

Schaff, Philip. *The Creeds of Christendom*. Vol. 3. New York: Harper & Brothers, 1882.

Scheers, G. Ph. *Philippus Jacobus Hoedemaker*. Wageningen: Drukkerij H. Veenman & Zonen, 1939.

Standard, The. Amsterdam: H. de Hoogh en Co., 1872–.

Stellingwerff, Dr. J. *Dr. Abraham Kuyper en de Vrije Universiteit*. Kampen: J. H. Kok, 1987.

Synopsis Purioris Theologiae . Leyden: Elsevier, 1625.

Teelinck, Willem. *Den politycken Christen. Ofte, Instructie voor alle hooge en leege Staetspersoonen*. Middelburg: Anthony de Later, 1650.

The Three Forms of Unity: Heidelberg Catechism, Belgic Confession, Canons of Dordrecht and the Ecumenical Creeds: the Apostles' Creed, the Athanasian Creed, the Creed of Chalcedon. n. p.: Mission Committee of the Protestant Reformed Churches of America, 1911.

Trigland, Jacobus. *Antapologia: sive examen refutatio totius apologiae Remonstrantium*. Amsterdam: Joannem Janssonium, 1664.

—. *Christelycke ende nootwendighe verclaringhe*. Amsterdam: Marten Iansz Brandt, 1619.

—. *Kerckelycke geschiedenissen* . Leyden: Adriaen Wyngaerden, 1650.

Udemans, Godefridum. *'t Geestelyck Roer van 't Coopmans Schip*. Dordrecht: François Boels, 1655.

Vermigli, Peter Martyr. *Loci Communes*. Heidelberg: Ioannem Lancellottum, 1553.

Voetius, Gijsbertus. *Politica Ecclesiastica*. 3 vols. Amsterdam: Johannem Janssonium, 1666.

—. *Schriftmatige en redenkundige verhandeling over de kerkelyke macht...* Rotterdam: Hendrik van Pelt & Adrianus Douci, 1756.

INDEX

www.ingramcontent.com/pod-product-compliance
Ingram Content Group UK Ltd.
Pitfield, Milton Keynes, MK11 3LW, UK
UKHW021627220925

8026UKWH00019B/209